Behind *Closed* Doors 2

Dana's Story

Revised Edition

BREAKING THE LINE BOOKS

Behind Closed Doors 2: *Dana's Story*
Revised Edition

Copyright © 2015 by A.L. Smith

ISBN – 13: 978-0692610787

This title is also available in e-book through Amazon and other retail outlets.

Visit www. alsmithbooks.com and www.breakingthelinebooks.com for more information.

All rights reserved. No part of this publication may be reproduced, stored in a retrieval system, or transmitted in any form or by any means – electronic, mechanical, photocopy, recording, or any other – except for brief quotations in printed reviews, without the prior permission of the publisher.

Any characters, occurrences, and/or places within this book are have no relation whatsoever to any persons, events, or places bearing the same name or names.

Library of Congress Control Number: 2015960934

Printed in the United States of America

ACKNOWLEDGEMENTS

Many thanks to God Almighty for giving me a vision and to my family for their never-ending support. This new journey is not an easy one, but I welcome the challenge.

I owe many thanks to a number of people, starting with my publisher A'Mera Frieman and Breaking the Line Books. Because of her, I understand the concept of "branding/re-branding" and the importance of "industry standard"...quality should always come first. To my personal street team, Amina Dyamond, Daniel Alexander, K. Anthony, Tanya Montena, and Michael Mack aka Lord Shabazz, thanks for your encouragement and words of inspiration. Huge thanks to Kamisha Bankston, Tracy Richardson and Catracy Goodman for reading my work ten years ago when it was in its early stages.

To my publicist, Michel by "Coco" Whitehead and Chocolate PR, Vaneka Miles Literary Services and Sistahs on Lit, patience is a virtue and a goal without a plan is simply a dream. Thanks guys!

Another huge thanks to Sheila Glenn (Fotosbysheila) for capturing the beautiful image and to Brittany Whitaker for gracing the cover of my book...it is indeed "picture perfect".

To my friends from elementary to high school, college and the U.S. Army, I love you all. And YES, the fictional HBCU in the Behind Closed Doors series (Gretna State University) was inspired by Dear Ole Grambling (GSU)...I still bleed Black and Gold. To Jabon, the amazing jazz band from Chi-town, with productive roots stemming from Grambling State University, thanks for providing the musical backdrop for me on many occasions...I was fortunate to discover your music on Tiger Roundup many years ago. Go GSU!!

I would be remiss if I didn't say "what's up" to Katrina Franklin, one of the busiest female entrepreneurs I know. After reading my first novel, she called me from one of her many destinations (Barbados, maybe?) to demand an advanced copy of Behind Closed Doors 2. Your words resonated.

A HUGE thanks to up and coming filmmaker/cinematographer/director Huey Rawls and So Nervy Films for bringing my characters to life. I asked for a book trailer and you gave me another goal (smile). To the cast members: Angel Smith, Brittany Whitaker, Kevin Tillet, Kayelyn Hawkins, Dewayne Michael, Tyrone Betters, Red Hightower, Prajwal Ramamurthy, and Hendrika Jacobs, thanks for rising to the occasion.

To Dr. and Mrs. Kikkeri and North Texas Team Care Surgery Center, thanks for your hospitality during our latest film project and your perpetual words of encouragement. I'm light years away from the greatness of Maya Angelou, but I appreciate the comparison.

Last but not least, to my readers, THANK YOU. The urban fiction market is an extremely competitive category and overflowing with an abundance of talented authors. You not only gave me a chance, but many of you took the time to reach out to me with words of encouragement. For that, I am eternally grateful. I would also like to thank you for your patience during my re-branding/re-launch process and your heartfelt anticipation for book three. I want you to know that I listen to my readers. As a result, this installment of Behind Closed Doors 2 is inclusive of the final installment--no cliff hangers, no book three. You have a finished product and a full length novel (Smile).

As an avid reader, I can say without a doubt, there is nothing new under the sun. As an author, my goal is to create characters that transcend the final pages of my books. My first novel, Behind Closed Doors 1, was written over a period of ten years, however, the majority of the time was spent writing the final chapters. As it turns out, life and the observation of life had to happen in order for me to finish. The Behind Closed Doors Series is my attempt to address some of the issues that we currently face in the urban community. Like most urban fiction novels, the perils of urban living (drugs, prostitution, child abuse/neglect, crime, police brutality, Black on Black crime and human trafficking) are discussed at length, but my primary goal is to explore the potential causes and effects...

"In a perfect world, we wouldn't have drug dealers and drug addicts wouldn't exist. Women wouldn't sell their bodies and every child would have both parents. Children would find value in education as opposed to tennis shoes, the neighborhood kingpin would NOT be a role model and ghettos would become obsolete in the absence of poverty. So, how did we get here? How did we allow the propaganda of superficial wealth to consume an entire generation?

"For the love of money is the root to all evil, but poverty and wealth are its greatest companions..." A.L. Smith

Behind Closed Doors: *Dana's Story* First Edition Reviews

Behind Closed Doors 2
Intelligently written story- not only did part 2 provide a profound storyline but gave me a vast amount of information concerning human trafficking, Louisiana/Haitian culture & drugs to name a few. It was disheartening that Dana's adolescent years were ruined by the person she loved & trusted the most. Dana's mother was just wicked & selfish! I loathed Mr. James! Ja'El & Miss Cookie were sent from above as they sincerely cared for Dana & played a healthy part in Dana's resilience to carry on...Tyree's appearance in Dana's life was important as he was a well taught lesson. Relevant background details & character appearances from part 1 made this story complete. Kudos to A.L. Smith for such an informative read that I highly recommend! ~ **Dee Cherry**

A.L. Smith did it again!!!!! Great read!!!
Another great read from an awesome author!!! I waited all day yesterday and I can honestly say the wait was worth it. I was gifted book one and I wanted to get Book 2 to show appreciation for a very talented author....A. L. Smith did it again she knocked it out the ballpark. I must say I did get emotional quite a bit to not really ever know what a mother's love feels like and to associate the wrong things with a man's love...I enjoyed this book and looking forward to Book 3. Kudos, Mrs. Smith, as some I know would say: You did that Miss Lady!!!!! ~ **Licia Samuel**

Well Done
A well written dramatics read. I am truly enjoying this series of book. The author is doing a great job keeping the stories flowing with great twist and turns that keep you hooked. ~ **Denetta Y. Banks**

Family Betrayal
The book was a good read. I don't understand how a mother would turn on her on child and use and abuse her. I would recommend this book. I want to see a Part three. ~ **Patricia Evans**

HUMAN TRAFFICKING

Domestic human trafficking is the central focus for Behind Closed Doors 2. According to the U.S. Department of Health and Human Services, human trafficking is no longer an international phenomena. It is the fastest growing criminal industry in the world today, second only to drug trafficking. The crime is reported over 200,000 times each year in the U.S. and the average entry age of minors into the sex trade is 12-14 years old. Many of the victims are runaway girls who have already suffered sexual abuse as children. Abject poverty, visible obscurity and numerous socioeconomic disparities are often the contributing factors. January is National Human Trafficking Awareness Month. The release of Behind Closed Doors 2 in the month of January is my personal attempt to raise awareness concerning the issue.

DEDICATION
Avalon Clark Borel
Rest easy, my friend.

Prologue

Dana

Fear is a defense mechanism that produces a vital response to emotional and physical danger.

Walking five blocks to and from school through the dangerous ghetto would have intimidated any twelve year old, but survival was a way of life and fear was my protection. There were no immediate signs of danger during my daily journey, but I was instinctively aware of everything around me and always prepared to act accordingly. As my classmates sped by me on their colorful bicycles, I grew excited about the prospect that I might finally get one of my own for Christmas. My father gave my mom the money to purchase the bike the previous year, but she used the money to pay the electric bill—at least, that's the story she told me. When I mistakenly allowed her to see my disappointment, I received a whipping and an hour-long speech about my ungratefulness.

"I feed you, and this is the thanks I get? I don't hear anyone else around here complaining and poor-mouthing," she said.

She looked at my younger sisters and my little brother for affirmation. I wanted to remind her of the fact that they had little to complain about since she gave them everything. My point was valid, but I was smart enough to know that a comment from me on the topic would result in another lashing.

My sisters didn't respond to the latest outburst from my mother because they were accustomed to it. However, I could see the paralyzing fear on their little faces. At times, the verbal and physical abuse that I received from my mother had a greater impact on them than it had on me. As a coping mechanism, I learned to channel everything to a place that was beyond the realm of feeling. I no longer responded to the physical pain that my mother inflicted and it drove her crazy. The verbal abuse escalated a few notches when she realized it had a greater effect on me than her physical punishments.

This was my life for as long as I could remember, but the intensity of the abuse dramatically increased when my parents separated. I was around eight years old at the time. When I got home from school that evening, I met my father at the front door. When I noticed the suitcases and plastic bags, my heart sank. I asked him if he was leaving for good and he said yes. My mother came out of the house in a violent rage, which worsened at the sight of my tears. Her eyes narrowed and she spoke to me through clenched teeth.

"Why don't you get your shit and go with your daddy! That's one less mouth for me to feed. I mean it, Bernard. Take that little hussy with you!"

She spoke as if her words were meant for a perfect stranger instead of her own daughter.

My father dropped his bags and knelt in front of me, without so much as even a glance toward my mother. He gave me a hug and cradled my face between his hands.

"I love you, Dana. Don't ever forget that," he said softly.

He gave me a hug and a kiss on the forehead, then turned to look at my mother for the last time. He spoke in Haitian Creole or "patois" to my mother, who was from South Louisiana. It was something my father often did to conceal his anger from me or whenever he wanted to discuss sensitive information with my mother. By now, I not only understood the language, but I spoke it fluently. Neither of my parents were aware of this. In his thick Haitian accent, he addressed my mother very calmly, but his anger was apparent.

"You're going to burn in hell for your evil ways, Diana," he said.

"I'll be waiting for you when you get there," she replied.

An evil smile crossed her face before she turned and walked back into the house.

My father left that day and my entire world crumbled.

Chapter One
For Better or Worse

My parents were born worlds apart, but they were connected in ways that still fascinate me to this day. Like Haiti, New Orleans was heavily influenced by the French during slavery. While many of the Louisiana and Haitian customs were diluted over the years, the Creole language and the practice of voodoo remained strong. A little known fact about the relationship between the two cultures was Haiti's role in the Louisiana Purchase. France was forced to sell its Louisiana territory to the United States after the Haitian Slave Revolution in 1803. France's finances were depleted during this conflict, as the French were no match for the ferocious Haitian warriors. As a result, Haiti is the only nation in the world established as a result of a successful slave revolt. My father was extremely proud of this fact and spoke of it often. Even more, he was proud of the fact that our family surname was the same as the given name of the dark-skinned Haitian general who orchestrated the revolt, Toussaint Louverture.

In addition to the similarities in the Creole language and the practice of voodoo, the similarities between Haitian and Louisianan culture are also strong when it comes to the issue of color. Social class was and still is to a certain degree, intricately tied to color. In both Haiti and Southern Louisiana, descendants of White male colonists and Black female slaves were allowed more rights than their darker counterparts. Mulattoes were often given their freedom and had access to economic and educational opportunities that were not available to their darker skinned counterparts. In south Louisiana, free mulattoes were allowed to live in prominent social and political communities separate from dark-skinned individuals. Endogamy or the practice of marrying within a specific group was common in places like New Orleans and the surrounding areas of South Louisiana. In order to maintain the color line, Mulatto children within these communities were forbidden to marry darker-skinned individuals. While endogamy is not a common practice in South Louisiana today, fragments of the sentiment still exist.

The profound link between the Haitian and South Louisianan cultures should have produced a perfect match for my parents, but my mother was the wild card. From all indications, her antiquated views about skin tone created a color barrier and heavily influenced her attitude toward my father and me. For the life of me, I couldn't think of any other reason for her behavior.

My father, Bernard Toussaint, was the proverbial tall, dark and handsome man, and there was a certain air about him that's hard to describe. When he entered a room, the attention immediately shifted in his direction and women just seemed to gravitate toward him. I guess you could say he had the perfect mixture of arrogance, confidence and strength, which separated him from everyone else.

My father was a Haitian-born immigrant, but not like the ones you read about in the news. He didn't travel to America on a boat like my mother often suggested when she was angry. His journey to this country was far more complex than that. My father's brother was a medical doctor and according to my father, he was absolutely brilliant. After completing medical school in Haiti, my uncle took the United States Medical Licensing Examination and obtained nearly perfect scores in the three-step examination process. He was accepted into a number of American schools but chose the University of Miami's orthopedic residency program due to its reputation and location.

After completing his training, my uncle built a hugely successful orthopedic surgical practice in Miami near an area called Little Haiti. Little Haiti was one of the poorest communities in south Miami, and well known for its drug-related criminal activities. In the late 80's and early 90's, corrupted Haitian officials played a major role in Colombian drug trafficking operations in south Florida and Little Haiti was the Mecca.

Once my uncle was established in Miami, he made some political connections that would allow him to bring immediate family members into the country if they so desired. My father was the only one to actually take advantage of the opportunity. This was something I never quite understood. If Haiti were anything like the American media's depictions, why would anyone pass up an opportunity to leave the country?

After making the transition to America, my father decided to further his education. He attended Miami-Dade community college for a few years with hopes of becoming an architect or graphic designer. However, contentment with student life in South Florida was virtually impossible due to the lures and trappings of quick money and the glamorous lifestyle. Eventually, he traded the student life in for the street life, which turned out to be a lucrative decision. The clean-cut college-boy appearance, coupled with the warrior spirit of his Haitian ancestors, facilitated his effortless transition into the world of drug trafficking. His success in the drug game was instant and he was clearly on his way to the top. In spite of the fact that he went through great lengths to conceal the nature of his new profession, my uncle eventually found out about it. At my uncle's urging, my father got out of the drug business and they both agreed that my father would have to leave South Florida in order to make a fresh start.

    With my uncle's assistance, he landed a carpentry job that would take him around the country constructing large corporate buildings and medical facilities. During a six-month stent in New Orleans, my father met and fell in love with my mother. When it was time to leave New Orleans and move on to the next job, he brought my mother with him to East St Louis and married her.

    My mother was a handful from the very beginning, but her spicy attitude was one of the things he loved most. He did everything in his power to make my mother happy, but it was never enough. Her desire for material possession overshadowed everything else. When my father realized he would never be able to meet my mother's financial expectations as a carpenter, he reverted back to his old ways and our living conditions improved immediately. He purchased a home for us in one of the few upscale neighborhoods in the city, complete with five bedrooms, four full bathrooms and a recreation room. Our house was laid with the finest of everything to include a bidet in the master bath. We had hardwood floors and ceramic tile throughout the entire house with several authentic Persian rugs strategically placed. The rugs were of the highest quality--silk on silk with wool in multi-color designs. All of the light fixtures and door handles were made from real brass and my mother insisted on custom wood blinds for every window. The kitchen was functionally beautiful with all of the up-to-date appliances to include two sets of expensive pots and pans--one set for daily use and the other set to hang beautifully from the ceiling at all times. The decor of our home was 19th century Victorian antique, which was a really popular design at the time. Unlike the typical knock-off replicas that were composed of plywood, my mother insisted on having every room filled with solid oak furnishings.

Like most of the affluent men in East St Louis, my father was a hustler. As a kid I didn't understand the meaning of the term. I just knew we had a good life compared to those around us. In addition to allowing my mother to stay laced in the finest that money could buy, he insisted on the same for my little brother, my sisters, and me. Everything we had was designer-made, from the ribbons in my hair to the Louis Vuitton book bag that I carried to school every day. My school uniforms didn't come from the local place where all of the other kids in the neighborhood got their uniforms. My uniforms were ordered directly from Land's End, an upscale school uniform company where the uppity, well-to-do families shopped for their kids. I also had a few custom designed outfits that were made for me by my father's seamstress. I guess he figured if he could wear custom designed suits, so could I. My mother didn't care one way or the other, as long as her wardrobe was tight. She spent most of her time taking trips across the river for her shopping expeditions. I was always relieved when she made those trips because she was always in a good mood when she returned.

My mother, Diana Ledoux Toussaint, was a very beautiful woman and she knew it. She also knew how to use it to her advantage. Both of my mother's parents were of French Creole descent and the mixing of their DNA resulted in my mother's appearance. My mother was one of those Southern belle type of ladies. She was short in stature, extra feminine, and her skin tone was almost light enough for her to pass the paper bag test. My mother had long, naturally curly hair that was jet-black. However, she wore it straight most of the time and colored it often so that she would "stand out" in the crowd. The small European nose, full lips and light hazel eyes gave her somewhat of an exotic appearance.

Because of her beauty, my mother was never concerned with education or a trade. Her only goal in life was to become a kept woman. I suppose this was a remnant of the old placage system, which was a way of life during New Orleans colonial days. Within this extramarital system, mulatto women were "kept" or "placed" with rich slave owners, who frequently established written contracts that provided property and sometimes freedom to the women and their offspring. Over time, the system contributed to a sense of entitlement for women like my mother.

My mother was born in a small back-woods town down on the Louisiana bayou, but she was raised in the projects of New Orleans. According to my mother, country living was too hard for my grandmother, who was left to raise four kids on her own after my grandfather was killed in a logging accident. My grandmother moved to the city and worked several jobs to take care of her family. The struggle was real, but she did it with dignity and took pride in the fact that she didn't have to rely on a man for her family's survival. She was very protective of her children and her primary goal was to keep as many negative influences out of their lives as she possibly could. It was not an easy task, for obvious reasons, but she did her best. My mother was always her biggest challenge.

The family moved around quite a bit at first. They lived in just about all of the run down housing developments in the city at one time or another, but my mother claimed the Ninth Ward as home. The Ninth Ward or "Desire Projects" was one of the roughest neighborhoods in the city. It was something my mother boasted about whenever she was in one of her gangster moods. According to her, East St Louis was nothing compared to the Ninth Ward. I suppose it's safe to say my mother was right at home in her new element.

Chapter Two
East St Louis aka "East Boogie"

Once upon a time, East St Louis was a thriving blue-collar town full of industrial jobs and promising opportunities for growth. Thousands of African-Americans made the journey North and settled in the city during the great migration in search of an alternative to the oppressive environment of the South. For years, the African-American middle class reaped the benefits bestowed upon the city. However, de-industrialization and restructuring of the railroad and meatpacking industry resulted in the precipitous loss of jobs and a profound reduction in income. The city was left with an aggregate of burned out buildings, run-down homes, a corrupt administration, and a robust drug trade.

East Boogie was a hustler's paradise and a junkie's dream...or nightmare, depending how you look at it. Heroin was the drug of choice when my father re-entered the game, but the introduction of crack cocaine to the city in the mid-80's gave birth to a new generation of addicts. For most of the clientele in East Boogie, powder cocaine was too expensive for habitual use, but the smokeable form of the drug was much cheaper. Due to the rapid decline in the cost of powder cocaine and the increasing demand for crack cocaine, every aspiring hustler in the city tried to come up.

Along with the hustle, came the violence. A majority of the violence in East St Louis was directly related to individual groups or gangs who were determined to establish locational rights through forced means. Turf violence in a city the size of East Boogie was a recipe for disaster, and the subsequent murders and drive-by shootings became a way of life.

Perhaps the most devastating effect of the crack epidemic was its impact on the children. The extremely addictive nature of crack cocaine, combined with its overwhelming appeal to women, contributed to the subsequent demise of the already fragile family structure. As a result, children became powerless victims of their circumstances and many of them were placed in the child welfare system.

My father was a major player from day one. At the peak of the violence and bloodshed, my father wanted out, but my mother wouldn't hear of it. The daily taunting and threats of "finding myself a real man" eventually became too much for him and he bounced. According to my mother, he ran back to Miami because he wasn't man enough to make her happy. This was the story that she told all of her friends. However, her friends were smart enough to know she'd made a huge mistake when she forced my father away.

Even though he was no longer with us, I knew my father still provided for us financially because my mother's bi-weekly shopping sprees never ceased. Her primary goal was to hook-up with another baller in order to maintain the lifestyle and reputation she'd worked too hard to build. Her priorities were obviously misplaced since her shopping sprees were more important than the mortgage payment. About a year after my father took off, we got a foreclosure notice in the mail and my mother was forced to get a job for the first time in her life. She became a custodian at the high school. The position wasn't what she really wanted, but at the time, she didn't have many options.

Unfortunately, her decision to get a job came a little too late and we were eventually forced out of our home. In spite of the long waiting list, my mother managed to get us into a small two-bedroom apartment in the projects. The waiting list for a larger apartment was at least three years long. For me, one of the craziest things about the move into the projects was the fact that my mom insisted on taking all of the expensive furniture and drapes with us. Our new home was laid, but the stuff was horribly misplaced in the dinky little apartment and most of the furniture pieces were too large to even fit. Even as a little kid, I was smart enough to question my mother's decision to keep the furniture. Why didn't she just sell it all to save the house? Of course, I knew the answer. For my mother, appearances were everything. She had to be surrounded by the best that money could buy, even in a modest environment. The furniture pieces that were too big to fit into the apartment were placed in a storage facility in hopes that she would have another house to put them in one day. The storage unit was around fifteen dollars every month, which was yet another bill and another reason for my mother's escalating frustration.

Her attitude toward me worsened after my father left, but her frustrations with our cramped living conditions compounded the problem. Money was a never-ending problem, but it was rarely an issue when it came to my little sisters and my brother. Their clothes were purchased directly from the department store while my clothes came from the local thrift shop. At times, my meals were even different from everyone else's and my lunch sack was always lighter. When I was around ten, I finally asked her if I was adopted because I just couldn't understand her behavior toward me. I fully expected some type of punishment for the question, but to my surprise, she just laughed it off and didn't bother to give an answer.

By that time, I was old enough to recognize the differences between my siblings and me. Dahlia and Dominique were carbon copies of my mother with slightly darker skin. My little brother, Omari Bernard, had a lot of my mother's features as well. However, at the age of two, Omari had all of my father's mannerisms and a seriousness that was totally out of place for his age. After three girls, my father was absolutely thrilled to finally have a son, and he wanted to name Omari after him. Of course, my mother was totally against this idea and Omari ended up with just a portion of my father's name as a compromise.

I, on the other hand, was definitely my father's child. I was tall for my age, and like him, I had a much darker complexion. The only feature I got from my mother was my hair. It wasn't as dark as hers, but it was about the same length and the texture was the same. When people saw us all together, they would make comments about the "beautiful little kids" and as an afterthought they would say things like, "Dana is really pretty for a dark skinned girl" or "I've never seen anyone as dark as you with such good hair." I hated when people talked about "good hair" because it made me feel uncomfortable. To me, the term was an insult to everyone that didn't have hair like mine. If soft and curly hair was "good hair," then coarse and kinky hair must be "bad hair." My mother had no problem with either of the terms or the concept. It was actually one of the things that contributed to her over-inflated ego.

Behind Closed Doors: *Dana's Story*

In addition to my struggles at home, I was forced to deal with my new surroundings. I'd lived a sheltered life in a beautiful home and a nice neighborhood, so I was totally unprepared for the projects. East St Louis was often referred to as the heart of America's bottom because of its location downstream from the Mississippi River. It was also considered one of the most impoverished small cities in the country. One of the things that separate third world countries from developed countries is a properly functioning sewerage system. On our first night in the projects, my mother had a fit when she noticed raw sewerage in the kitchen sink. The same thing happened on her job twice in one week. Sewerage backed up into the food prep area in the school cafeteria, and the students were sent home indefinitely until repairs were made.

Other signs of third world living conditions in East Boogie were just as appalling. Since the city was unable to maintain the salaries of the sanitation workers, trash services were suspended indefinitely and residents burned their own trash or allowed it to pile up in their yards. As a result, rodent life was completely out of control, and reports of rats as big as small puppies occurred on a daily basis. Ironically, East St Louis was home to one of the nation's largest hazardous waste and incineration companies in the country. No joke.

With a population of less than thirty thousand residents, the city had one of the highest murder rates in the country, comparable to cities like New York, New Orleans, DC, Detroit and Baltimore. The vicious cycle of poverty and substance abuse was the greatest contributing factor to the violence. Substandard education and few job opportunities made it extremely hard to sustain even the basic necessities of life. Kids were placed in survival mode at an early age and learning how to survive was like learning how to breathe. The only ambition for most of the boys was to get into the drug game and to hook up with a baller was every girl's dream.

In addition to the drug trade, the city's nightlife was legendary. The club scene was actually responsible for the city's moniker, "East Boogie". Going to the club was serious business for residents of East Boogie and my mother lived for it. She was a baller wife and my father was the biggest baller in the city. All of that changed when he left. In all honesty, the loss of her status was probably harder for her to deal with than the loss of my father.

Chapter Three
The Unthinkable

It was the week after Thanksgiving and I was already excited about Christmas. The festive lights and decorations were already up and flashed beautiful amidst the empty wine bottles, crack vials, and plastic baggies that sporadically covered the sidewalks. While the decorations seemed a little out of place, they were still a welcomed sight in the unpleasant environment known as my hood. My pace through the neighborhood was unusually slow on that particular day and I paid extra attention to the scenery.

In the nicer area of the neighborhood, the yards were neater and well kept. These particular houses stood out like mini mansions amongst the other run-down homes in the area, but none of the homes were as nice as the home that we once had on the other side of town. Miss Bertha, the neighborhood gossip was on her porch. As usual, she looked for anything out of the ordinary to report to the person on the other end of her phone. Next door, Mr. and Mrs. Hawkins stood outside their picket fence and waited for their son Josh, who was a couple of years older than me. A row Section 8 houses were situated just beyond the Hawkins' home. These houses were okay, but they were clearly not as nice as the ones on the previous block. My mother's primary goal in life was to hook up with another baller, but her other goal was to move our family into one of the Section 8 houses. Unfortunately, this would be next to impossible with all of the other families on the waiting list.

As I made my way up the stairs to our apartment, I took a deep breath and prepared myself for my mother's evening tirade. To my surprise, when I walked into the house there was silence. She just glared at me for a moment and then she spoke.

"Go to your room and change clothes, Dana--don't take all day," she said quietly.

"Okay momma. What do you want me to put on?"

"I don't care what you put on. Just hurry up and change."

The irritation was apparent in her voice, so I took a deep breath and hurried to my room to take off my school uniform. I took my time because I wasn't in a hurry to find out the latest source of her irritation. When I heard the knock at the door, I was relieved because I thought it was my mother's friend, Miss Cookie. Miss Cookie was always a God-send because whenever she was around, my mother focused less of her attention on me. To my surprise, I heard a man's voice and it was unfamiliar. I was disappointed but relieved all the same because a distraction of any sort was better than the alternative...or so I thought.

After I changed out of my school uniform into a pair of jeans and a pullover sweater, I went back into the living room. My mom was at the kitchen table with a man I'd never seen. Creepy is the only way to describe him because of the way his eyes seemed to follow me around the room. He was extremely well-dressed and very handsome. I guessed he was probably in his late thirties to mid-forties.

"Dana, you're going for a ride with Mr. James. I want you to be good and do whatever he tells you to do, you understand?"

"But momma I don't..."

My heart pounded in fear, and after moment, I gathered the courage to protest. She cut me off immediately.

"Look, don't talk back to me. Just do what I say," she said.

I looked at my mom and then at Mr. James. I couldn't think of any reason for me to be going anywhere with this strange man. However, I didn't have much of a choice. When we reached the front door, I turned back to look at my mother one last time. She just stood there with her arms folded and her face without any expression.

I followed Mr. James to a fancy black car and he opened the door for me. I wanted to ask him where we were going but I was too afraid to say anything. We stopped at a convenience store and I waited in the car while he went inside. He came back with a bag full of candy and a jungle juice. When we pulled back into the traffic, I noticed that we were headed in the direction of my old house and I got excited. Maybe my prayers had been answered. Was he here to take me to my father? That's what was going through my mind when we pulled into the driveway of the gigantic house with the electric fence.

The strange man didn't speak a word to me during the entire trip. When he stopped the car, I looked at him and waited for him to say something--anything. I wanted to know what was going on.

He said nothing and neither did I. We went into the house and he disappeared. I was left to stand in the foyer. I stood there and admired the beautiful paintings and statues. It was the nicest house I'd ever seen. I wondered if the man actually lived there. If so, where was his family? Surely he didn't live there alone. As I stood there and contemplated the various possibilities, I prayed that the man would return with my father and that he would tell me this was my new home. That would not be the case. Mr. James returned dressed in a silk robe and slippers. He took my hand and led me to the kitchen, then gestured for me to take a seat on the wood and iron barstool. He briefly touched my hair and began a brief line of questioning.

"So, Dana, how old are you?"

He spoke softly as he pulled me closer.

"I'm twelve."

My heart beat faster with fear.

"That's pretty young, but I think you're old enough to learn this game I'm about to teach you. You like playing games?"

"Yes, Mr. James".

"Then, you'll love this one. Follow me."

I followed him through the kitchen and the huge living room, which looked like a page from an interior designs magazine. Everything was perfect and every object appeared to be in its proper place. The master bedroom completely took the cake. It was bigger than our entire apartment and everything was snow white, including the furniture and drapes. He told me to sit on the sofa, but I continued to stand for fear that I would stain the beautiful piece of furniture. He disappeared again, this time he returned with a banana, a plate, and a bottle of chocolate syrup. He placed the banana onto the plate, peeled it, and poured chocolate syrup on it as he explained the rules to the "game."

My job was to lick all of the chocolate syrup from the banana without allowing my teeth to touch it. It seemed easy enough and I loved chocolate, but the whole thing was just weird. When I was finished, he took off the silk robe and stepped out of the leopard print silk boxers.

"Have you ever seen a man's banana?"

Behind Closed Doors: *Dana's Story*

His voice sounded weird when he asked the question. I didn't say anything. He proceeded to place a towel beneath his genitalia and squirted chocolate all over his private area. In order to win the prize, I had to do what I'd just done to the real banana. I refused and began to cry. Everything began to make sense and I panicked. Did my mother know that she'd placed me into the hands of a man who obviously had a thing for little girls?

Clearly irritated with my reaction, he disappeared again. This time, he returned with another plate. This one had three straight lines of a white powdery substance on it. Within seconds, one of the lines was gone and he placed the plate in front of me.

"Your turn, Dana," he said with an evil grin.

He didn't give me a chance to respond. He pushed my head down on the plate, and with each breath, I inhaled the substance. There was an instant effect. All of a sudden, I was floating and I had this overwhelming sense of well-being. The anxiety I'd felt since I left home was replaced by an indifference to everything around me. Next thing I knew, he was in front of me with the bottle of chocolate. When the deed was done and the rush from the cocaine was gone, I just wanted to lie down. I woke up a couple of hours later in the middle of the huge bed. Mr. James sat comfortably across the room in a beautiful oversized chaise lounge. I felt deathly ill with a horrible belly ache and I panicked. I didn't think Mr. James would be pleased if I puked all over his white linen sheets.

"I don't feel well, Mr. James."

I moaned and grabbed my belly with one hand and covered my mouth with the other.

"Go to the bathroom, Dana," he said and gestured a hand toward the door.

I bolted from the bed and ran as fast as I could. I made it to the toilet just before everything in my body came out. When I returned to the bedroom, Mr. James was fully dressed.

"Go to the kitchen and wait for me," he said.

He picked up the phone to place a call and dismissed me.

In the kitchen, I noticed the table was set and there were two plates of food. Although I wasn't feeling well, I thought about my last meal, which had been at school during lunch. The salami and cheese sandwich was long gone and I was hungry. Since I didn't know if either of the plates was meant for me, I just sat down in one of the chairs opposite from the two plates of food and waited.

"Why aren't you eating Dana? Your mother told me about your healthy appetite. Said she can't keep enough food on the table for you."

Really, I thought, but I didn't say anything. I moved to the other side of the table and dug in. Spaghetti was my favorite. I wondered if he'd cooked it himself. As if he'd read my mind, he confirmed my thoughts.

"I made it especially for you. Your mom said it was your favorite."

I was nearly done, but that last comment completely spoiled my appetite. He seemed to know an awful lot about me.

"Are you finished?"

He noticed that I'd put my fork down.

"Yes, sir," I said and kept my eyes lowered.

"Then, I guess it's time to get you home."

I had never experienced a desire to get home to my mother, but at that moment, it was the only place I wanted to be. I was relieved when he turned into our complex. When the car finally came to a stop, I jumped out and ran up the stairs. After I banged on the door for what seemed like forever, my mother finally appeared. I ran past her and my sisters to get to the bathroom and nearly knocked my little brother over when he turned the corner. For the second time that night, my stomach responded violently to the evil things that took place. All of the spaghetti and garlic bread came up, and I started to sweat profusely, but I was cold at the same time. My mother stood in the doorway for a moment with an alarmed look on her face and then returned to the living room with Mr. James.

Once I finished depositing the rest of the meal into the toilet, I tipped out of the bathroom and peeped around the corner. I couldn't believe my eyes. Mr. James placed three one hundred dollar bills into my mother's hand and she smiled. That's when I knew for certain that my mother was aware of everything that took place that evening. There was no need for me to tell her anything. She had a business arrangement with a pervert and I provided the services.

Behind Closed Doors: *Dana's Story*

I sat on the floor in the hallway until Mr. James left and waited for her to say something. At this point, it didn't really matter what she said, I just wanted her to say something.

"Go take your bath. You have school tomorrow," she said.

That was it. I guess it wasn't really what she said; it was what she didn't say. She didn't ask if I was ok or if he hurt me. She said absolutely nothing. Her indifference to me and what happened that night proved beyond a shadow of doubt what I'd felt my entire life. My mother didn't love me. How could you love someone and cause them harm at the same time? When I got home from school the next day, Miss Cookie was there to babysit. My mother took the afternoon off from her job to go shopping. It was as if nothing ever happened.

To my dismay, it happened again the following week. When I got home from school, my mother told me to change clothes, and Mr. James showed up shortly after. Like last time, no words were exchanged between us and we made another quick stop at the convenience store for my favorite snacks.

When we reached our destination, my heart sank. This time, he took me to the kitchen as soon as we arrived. There was food on the stove. I was instructed to fix myself a plate and to eat all of it. A trip to the bedroom, two lines of coke, and the banana game followed dinner.

The Tuesday night ritual continued for a few weeks, but it didn't take long for the games to evolve into something more sinister than just chocolate and bananas. Each degrading act was worse than the previous one, but more palatable with each line of coke. After a few months of consistent use, coke became my friend. At thirteen, I had an insatiable taste for the substance. I looked forward to the instant euphoria and the sense of peace that came over me. It gave me the ability to accept the unacceptable and it numbed the physical and mental pain that I was forced to endure.

Surprisingly, the only thing that kept me from taking the final plunge into addiction was Mr. James. He was my supplier, but he also controlled my usage of the substance. I was forbidden to use it outside of his presence and I complied. It was just as well, since I didn't have the resources to obtain it on my own anyway.

Behind Closed Doors: *Dana's Story*

I spent my thirteenth birthday watching skin flicks with Mr. James. It didn't take me long to realize he was grooming me for the next level of abuse. Watching the video was an extremely traumatic experience for me because it provided a window into my future. Even worse, it killed any optimism I had about the possibility of an end-point to the whole thing. Perhaps I was selfish, but I prayed that he would find interest in some other little girl and leave me alone. My prayers went unanswered again, and the inevitable occurred just a few days later.

At first the visits were just once a week, but it quickly became three days a week-- rain, shine, sleet or snow. For each encounter, my mother received three hundred dollars. The grand total was thirty-six hundred a month. It was enough for my mother to quit her job at the school and move us into a larger apartment outside of the projects.

With so much free time on her hands, she decided to go to beauty school. Once she finished school, she set up shop in one of the more popular salons in the city and became an instant success. I prayed that she would make enough money to finally put an end to the little business arrangement that she had with Mr. James, but it never happened. My mother was addicted to money, clothes, jewelry, and status. Although she didn't speak on it much, from time to time, she reminded me of the fact that her arrangement with Mr. James was necessary because our family needed the money. According to her, I had to pull my weight so to speak or "take up the slack for your sorry ass daddy," she would tell me.

To say that I lost respect for my mother would be extremely mild. There were no words to describe the anger and betrayal that I felt towards her each time I returned home and witnessed the exchange of money between her and Mr. James. The "rewards" for me, which included hot meals and new outfits on a pretty frequent basis, would have the greatest impact on my views related to life and men. At thirteen, sexual favors were synonymous with material gain.

At fourteen, I was pregnant. As a true indication of my immaturity, this was something I never even considered a possibility. By then, Mr. James was not the only pervert in my life. Several of his friends paid him a hefty fee for a few moments of my time. According to Mr. James, the possibility that he was the father of my baby was extremely low. I never really understood how he could be so sure of this, but I took it for what it was worth. I suppose his reasons didn't matter one way or the other. Because of all of the other potential sperm donors, the paternity of my child would be a mystery regardless.

My mother blamed me of course, which made no sense whatsoever. How could any of this be my fault? She was the one to blame because she put me in the situation in the first place and took no precautions to prevent it from happening. She had to know that sex was involved, so why didn't she put me on the pill? Her only concern was to keep the pregnancy a secret, which luckily for her, turned out to be easier than she expected. No one knew I was pregnant because I didn't gain very much weight until the seventh month. When I couldn't hide it anymore, she sent me to Louisiana to live with my grandmother until the baby was born.

When I got there, my grandmother took one look at me and shook her head. After that, she grabbed me and hugged me so hard I could barely breathe. My grandmother was the total opposite of my mother. She loved me and I knew it. I looked forward to the two weeks we spent with her each summer because it was the only time I could actually be a kid.

"Diana, how could you let this happen? Why didn't you just send her to me?" my grandmother asked.

"Look momma, you can't watch these little fast girls twenty-four hours a day. I did the best I could, so don't blame me for this. Blame her sorry ass daddy for leaving me with all of the bills and four mouths to feed," my mother said.

She basically threw me under the bus and pretended to be the helpless single mother. Yet she stood there with no less than a thousand dollars invested in the clothes, shoes and the purse she carried. Unbelievable. I just looked at her. At that moment, I acknowledged the fact that I hated her with everything in me.

My mother came from a huge extended family. As a result, I had too many cousins to even count. My cousin Lenny Jr. and his sisters were my favorite. Lenny's father was my mother's oldest brother. While my mother and Uncle Leonard were often mistaken for twins, they were polar opposites. He was decent and respectable. My mother was pure evil. I came close to telling my uncle and my cousins about my ordeal, but I was too ashamed and afraid of being ridiculed for not speaking up sooner. I totally regretted my decision. Had I spoken up, perhaps I would have avoided the pregnancy dilemma.

Per my mother's instructions, we couldn't tell anyone about my pregnancy. My grandmother and I did our best to honor her request, but we didn't really understand her rationale. People would find out sooner or later--or so we thought. My mother showed up a couple of days before I went into labor. Instead of taking me to a hospital, she took me to someone's house in the projects and a "midwife" delivered my baby. He was born on March 16, 1987. After a brief glimpse of my son, my mother whisked him away. When I asked to see him the next day, she told us about the adoption. I could see the color drain from my grandmother's fair-skinned face and at first she didn't say a word. When she finally spoke, the anger and rage was quietly apparent.

"I didn't raise you this way, Diana. What happened to you?"

She spoke softly in patois. When my mother didn't respond, my grandmother went to her room and closed the door. My mother and I could hear her cry, but neither of us moved or said a word.

From what I could remember, my son was absolutely beautiful. He had cocoa brown skin, mounds upon mounds of soft curly hair, and his eyes were identical to mine. Even though my child was conceived under unspeakable circumstances, I still loved him and I felt like a piece of my heart was torn away. When I compared my thoughts and feelings toward my child to my mother and her actions toward me, I was even more confused. The bond between a mother and her child is supposed to be the strongest type of bond between humans and almost every other species known to man. I was living proof that this concept is not completely infallible. I never saw my son again.

There was complete silence during the eight-hour drive back to East Boogie. The anger and rage I had toward my mother grew with each passing mile. By the time we reached home, I decided I'd had enough. I could no longer live under the same roof or breathe the same air as this woman. When my mother left the house the next day, I packed my things and left. Miss Cookie had

Behind Closed Doors: *Dana's Story*

always been more like a mother to me than my own mother, but I wasn't sure if she would welcome me into her home. However, I was prepared to beg if I had to.

To my surprise, she didn't ask any questions when I showed up on her doorstep with three large trash bags and my schoolbooks. She simply took me to her spare bedroom and told me to get some rest. I wasn't sure if she knew about Mr. James, but I had a feeling she knew about the baby. I wanted to confide in Miss Cookie, but I couldn't. Again, the shame, guilt, and humiliation prevented me from speaking out about such a horrible situation. Yes, it could have fixed all of my problems, but what if she didn't believe me? Or even worse, what if she blamed me? I continued to deal with it in silence. There was no way to change what already happened. There were too many secrets and unanswered questions. How do you come to terms with the fact that your mother is actually your pimp? And where was my father so that I could tell him what was happening? Did anyone care that Mr. James had a sick attraction for little girls?

While there was very little spoken communication between Mr. James and me, one day he made his feelings about my father known. As it turns out, he hated my father. I couldn't help wondering if his feelings toward my father had anything to do with his decision to ruin my life.

The bright side to the situation was that I didn't have to deal with him anymore. Since I no longer lived with my mother, the deal was officially over, or so I thought. About a week after I gave birth to my son, I went back to school and struggled to catch up. I was determined not to fail the ninth grade. After my first day back in school, Mr. James showed up at Miss Cookie's. The knock at the door startled me at first, but not enough to make me look through the peephole before I opened the door. When I opened the door and realized it was him, I nearly fainted. He grabbed me by the hand and proceeded to threaten me indirectly.

"So, this is where you've been hiding. I went by your house the other day and you weren't there. Your mother suggested I check over here," he said softly.

He stroked my hair, which was slightly damp from a long hot shower. I didn't say anything, so he continued.

"Your little sisters are growing up to be beautiful little ladies, Dana, but they'll never be as beautiful as you," he said.

My plan was to resist or threaten to go to the police or do anything to put an end to our "relationship," but his words stopped me in my tracks. His message was clear. If I didn't continue to cooperate, my sisters could be next. On the one hand, I didn't think my mother would allow it because she loved them. On the other hand, my mother was a selfish bitch and I couldn't take the risk.

"Where are we going?"

I turned up my lip in disgust.

"Mi Casa. Where else?"

He sneered and licked his lips.

So, less than a month after I gave birth to a child who was literally taken from my arms and whisked away to God knows where, my nightmare resumed. Nothing changed except the fact that I no longer lived with my mother. In spite of this, she continued to receive compensation for my services. Living with Miss Cookie was the best thing that ever happened to me, and I'm sure my mother felt the same way. It meant she rarely had to face me or look me in the eye and I didn't have to look at her. To keep Miss Cookie out of her business, my mother came up with a cover story to explain my absences during the week and Mr. James began to pick me up around the corner from the school on Monday, Wednesday and Friday.

Chapter Four
MOET--Money over Every Thing

It was springtime in East Boogie and I was approaching the end of my junior year. It was beautiful outside, I thought, as I made my way down the street to my best friend's house for our daily walk to school. I was wearing yet another new outfit, so I expected at least one run-in with my haters--it never failed. But I was used to it. I had long given up trying to be civil; instead, I learned to fight back. I was pretty good with my hands and I carried something sharp on me at all times and in multiple places. The smart females knew not to mess with me, but there were still a few brave ones left for me to contend with.

"Dana its Friday and you've been rolling up in here with fresh gear every day. What's up with that?" Ja'El (pronounced Yah' Ell) asked. She was checking out my new Jordan's, the all-white Girbaud jeans and denim shirt I was wearing. She was right. I was rocking new outfits like crazy since Mr. James got me the hook-up at the strip club. I was also receiving a little salary on the side from some of Mr. James' friends. I was literally balling out of control and everyone knew it. However, they didn't know my struggle or the source of my income. At some point, I conceded to my fate and allowed the money to reconcile the differences. I was officially a product of my environment. My mind and my body no longer belonged to me--they belonged to the streets. With very few options to choose from, I chose money over everything else.

Ja'El was my only friend because all of the other girls hated me. In the early days, it was because of my hair; however now, they hated me for my seemingly perfect life. I was the flyest girl in the whole school, hands down, and the fellows were checking for me on the regular. Even the ones who had girlfriends made it perfectly clear to everybody that if I ever looked twice, it was on and popping. Little did the females know, I was the least of their problems. Their so-called boyfriends were mentally and physically incapable of handling a girl like me and I didn't have time to give lessons.

The snub from the females at school bothered me a little at first, but I figured since I couldn't change the way they felt about me, I had to roll with it. Ja'El had been rolling with me since middle school, and like most of the kids in our school, she had serious issues at home as well. Ja'El's mom was a crack head and she was well known around town for doing any and everything for her next hit. One day, I walked up on some girls giving Ja'El a hard time about her mother and the odds were clearly not in her favor. Ja'El had a reputation for being tough, but she was no match for this group. I made a split second decision to intervene. A quick flash of the box cutter that I was carrying took care of it. The three chicken heads scattered like roaches and Ja'El and I became allies for life.

On this particular day, our friendship was put to the test.

"You know, Dana, I think I finally figured you out. You won't let me in on your little hustle because you wanna keep it all for yourself. Some kind of friend you are," she said and walked away.

As close as we were, Ja'El didn't know my whole story, and needless to say, I was a little hesitant about telling her. In the past, whenever she questioned me about the source of my seemingly "good fortune," I simply changed the subject. She'd give me the cold shoulder for a few days but she always came around. Today was different. I sensed a little desperation in her voice.

"Ja'El!"

I screamed in panic at the thought of losing the only friend I had. When I caught up with her, she was crying crocodile tears.

"Really, Ja'El? It's that important to you?"

I asked, feeling torn and irritated about the situation.

Ja'El was a good girl and she was probably the smartest kid in the entire school. Although I had to admit, being the smartest kid in the school wasn't really saying much considering the schools in East Boogie. They were a joke like everything else in the city, but Ja'El had always taken it seriously. Her only downfall was being born to a mother who was more concerned about her next rock than she was about her own daughter. Ja'El was the baby of the family and she'd watched her mother and her uncles become totally debilitated by crack cocaine. Ja'El had two older brothers, but they lived with their respective fathers. If it hadn't been for her grandmother, Ja'El would have been left to fend for herself. But Ja'El had a plan. She was going to some college down in Louisiana after high school. She planned to leave East Boogie and never look back.

That was my primary reason for keeping Ja'El in the dark about my situation. I didn't want her to get side tracked. The baller life was extremely appealing to people in the hood, but looks were deceiving. The type of money that I made and my lifestyle wasn't the type of thing to hang your hat. It would be easy for someone like Ja'El to get caught up in the fast money and I didn't want her dreams to get derailed by the trappings of the street. I was in a serious 'Catch 22'. My only friend in the whole freaking world was calling me selfish. How was I going to get her to see that a new pair of Jordan's and a banging wardrobe wasn't worth the sacrifices that I had to make to attain them? The look of betrayal and desperation that she gave forced me to come clean. I told her everything. I started at my mother's abuse and her arrangement with Mr. James. I described my relationship with Mr. James in detail, and explained how the arrangement evolved into other moneymaking opportunities. I even told her about my ever increasing love for powder cocaine and the son that I would probably never see again. To say the words out loud for the first time seemed to breathe life into the situation. It was like I emerged from a horrible dream and woke up in harsh reality. By the time that I finished giving her all of the gory details, we were both in tears.

"That's why you never smile," she said quietly while we both sat on the park bench and cried.

She was right, I couldn't recall ever having a reason to smile after my father left, but I didn't think anyone noticed.

"Dana, your mom isn't on drugs or anything, is she?"

Ja'El asked while dumbfounded by my revelation.

"Yah-Yah, my mother hates drugs. She can barely stand the smell of weed. This may sound crazy, but I would actually feel better if she was a crackhead. Money is her only addiction. She basically used me to maintain her lifestyle."

"I'm so sorry, Dana. My mom has been strung out since I was three and she's never done anything like this. Your mother is the worst kind of evil and she's going to pay for what she did to you. Dana, I knew about the baby. When you went away, I assumed you had an abortion."

"How did you know?"

"You're like a sister to me, Dana. How could I not know?"

"But you never said anything."

"I just figured you would tell me when you got around to it."

"I couldn't talk about it, Yah. It was just too hard. I go to sleep with him on my mind and he's the first thing I think about when I wake up. It's a horrible feeling."

Ja'El was right. What my mother did to me was criminal, but I didn't know what to do about it, nor did I have the courage to do anything. I didn't know it then, but I eventually discovered the name of the crime. It's called "familial human trafficking".

Most people consider human trafficking an international phenomenon with images of women from third world countries. However, another category of victims that most people are clueless about, include individuals born on American soil to circumstances beyond their control. I came across the term while killing time in the city library. I spent hours reading everything I could get my hands on concerning the topic. What I discovered was astounding. Eighty-three percent of all human trafficking cases in this country involve American children. The victims are often hidden in plain sight and the diabolical acts are obscured by poverty, crime, and drug infested surroundings. Due to the poor infrastructure, illegal drug activity, crime, and poverty, East Boogie was the epitome of a third world country. Therefore, it was an ideal setting for this type of crime.

The child welfare system in East Boogie was a joke when it came to the issue. Mandatory reporting of suspected child abuse was virtually unheard of or ignored because the shortage of child protection workers in the city was at an all-time high. As a result, girls caught in the midst of this type of illegal activity were usually placed in the juvenile justice system and ultimately punished for crimes in which they were the actual victims. This was all first-hand information for me. I'd been arrested for suspicion of solicitation while hanging outside at the strip club and I was headed straight to juvie court. Mr. James and his connections with crooked law enforcement agents in the city was the only thing that saved me. The twisted part about the whole thing was the fact that he was responsible for my presence there in the first place and should have faced charges. Even more twisted was the fact that the prospect of entering the juvenile justice system was more appealing to me than my current predicament.

In essence, America's sex slave market is very similar to those found in places like Cambodia, India, and the Philippines, with only a few minor differences. For example, victims of familial human trafficking aren't stolen or placed in completely unfamiliar territory. American victims are often exploited in familiar territory and on the surface they carry on seemingly "normal" lives. In addition, the traditional pimp is replaced by trusted individuals or those least expected to harm the child: parents, step-parents, foster parents, etc. The abusers are often known to the victims and may include individuals such as the janitor at the school or one of the deacons in the church. In spite of the differences between domestic and international human trafficking, poverty is typically the common denominator, however, greed is a close second. In places where primitive needs like food, clothes, and shelter are lacking and survival is the daily objective, sexual servitude becomes a viable option.

Behind Closed Doors: *Dana's Story*

Chapter Five
Thinkin' of a Master Plan

"Dana, here's the deal. I can't spend the rest of my life in this hell hole. I'm going to college, if it's the last thing I do. The problem is, Pell grants and financial aid won't cover the out of state fees and all of the other expenses. I'm not trying to do this for clothes and shoes and all of that other stuff. I need you to put me on because it's the only option I have. In a few months, we'll be seniors and it'll be time for me to shit or get off the pot. I need at least twenty grand to get me through the first year. Where the hell am I gonna get that kind of loot?"

According to Ja'El, a gig at the strip club would solve all of her financial problems. Of course, she was right. The potential earnings would be more than enough for her to achieve her financial goals and she could finally execute her plan of escape. How could I say no?

There were two main adult entertainment clubs in East Boogie: the Whiz and the Oz. I didn't think we'd have any problems getting her into the Whiz, which was the strip club that catered to Black clientele. However, the Oz was a gold mine and to get a job there would be much harder. The Oz was located directly across the street from the Whiz and it was reserved for the White yuppie crowd that ventured across the bridge in search of a good time. I started out at the Whiz, where I was free to hone my newly acquired skills. Once Mr. James was convinced that I was ready, he took me across the street to meet the owner of the Oz. He was immediately taken by my "exotic looks." By now, I was painfully aware of my appeal to dirty old men and I'd resigned myself to the fact that it was a gift. I figured I might as well be paid to use it. I was five foot nine inches tall and a buck twenty five. My large c-cup boobs were a perfect fit for my extra small waist and 36 inch hips. There was very little work for me to do in order to seal the deal. I simply sashayed in a little circle for the owner and paused for a second so that he could adequately assess my backside. I was hired on the spot. After I learned a few white girl tricks for the pole, I was bringing in no less than two grand a week on Saturday nights alone and Mr. James was paid a nice little "finder's fee" for my

Behind Closed Doors: *Dana's Story*

services. Strangely, for the first time in my life I actually felt good about myself.

Since I couldn't talk Ja'El out of her aspiration of becoming a stripper, I had to figure out how to get her in the door. Her body was banging enough, but she looked like a kid with the little asymmetrical hairstyle and headbands. After brainstorming for a couple of days, I came up with the perfect solution.

After school that day, I took her across the bridge to a beauty salon that specialized in hair extensions. I paid for a fourteen-inch sew-in and left Ja'El in the capable hands of Miss Henrietta, the stylist. I proceeded on to the little spot where I purchased my "Dorothy gear," which was what I called my club outfits. I guess it was my way of paying homage to the Wizard of Oz, since the gig had become my "yellow brick road". Like Ja'El, my goal was to get out of the hood as well. I wasn't exactly sure how I was gonna do it, but I knew I would need a substantial amount of money to make it happen.

When I made it back to the salon, I was floored by the results. Miss Henrietta was a beast with a needle and thread. Ja'El's transformation was everything I needed it to be and more. You couldn't even tell it was a weave. Ja'El couldn't stop staring at herself in the mirror. I finally had to drag her out of the shop.

Our next stop was the Whiz and like expected, she was in-- no questions asked. But I was still a little nervous about Oz. I was sure it would cause major problems between Ja'El and me if they rejected her and I wasn't in the mood to deal with another argument. I took a deep breath, thought about my little sales pitch, and we walked in to see the owner. I wanted to take a stab at making things happen on my own, without the assistance of Mr. James. I didn't know if it was gonna work, but it was worth a try if it meant keeping Ja'El on the pole and away from Mr. James and his foul friends.

The owner of the club, Mr. Jerry, took one look at Ja'El and he was sold. I refused the "finder's fee", which was customary for ladies who were guaranteed moneymakers. In exchange, he promised not to discuss the arrangement with Mr. James. This was an additional measure that I put into place to ensure that Mr. James wouldn't try to cash in on Ja'El's profit, or even worse, I didn't want him to try to get her on his payroll.

Behind Closed Doors: *Dana's Story*

Friday night was one of my standing "date nights" with Mr. James. After all of our business transactions were complete, I left Ja'El's and took the dreaded walk to the other side of town. Mr. James was livid, just as I expected.

"Where the hell have you been Dana? I waited for you for over an hour and you know I don't like waiting!"

"I had to stay over for a tutoring class."

The lie rolled off of my tongue with ease.

"We're preparing for one of those standardized tests and they're trying to make sure we're ready. This is my last chance to pass the test. If I fail, I won't graduate."

I threw that part in for good measure. I'd already taken the test and passed months ago.

"You know I want you to do well in your school work, but you need to let me know about things like this in advance. I was worried."

Surprisingly, he bought the story. I was convinced at that moment that there had to be a name for this type of perversion. In spite of the fact that he'd been my abuser since I was twelve years old, there were times when he had the nerve to be fatherly. I must have been just as insane as he was because in spite of everything he'd done to me, there were times when I felt safer in his presence than anywhere else.

Over the years, Mr. James became a little lax around me with his personal chitchat. As a result, I finally figured out his occupation. In addition to his fetish for little girls, he was a major player in East Boogie's dope game. He was also my father's biggest rival back in the day. When my father left, Mr. James assumed the role as East Boogie's ghetto king. As it turns out, my earlier suspicions were correct. His interest in me was partially related to his hatred of my father and his actions were rooted in revenge. For some twisted reason, my mother assisted him to make it all possible. In a way, I sort of understood Mr. James' motivation, but I would never understand my mother's willingness to place me into the hands of the enemy. I felt like a pawn in a never-ending game of chess.

When I made it back to Miss Cookie's around midnight, I was surprised to find her still awake. She sat on her sofa and puffed on her doobie with her eyes closed. Her favorite drink, Crown Royal, was nearby and Al Green boomed loudly from the speakers. When I was younger, I actually thought Miss Cookie was married to Al Green because of the way she carried on about him.

"Sha la la la la la, oh baby," she sang loudly and snapped her fingers to the beat.

I could tell she was in a good mood, but I braced myself for the lecture that I thought was sure to come regarding the time. Instead, she spoke the words I'd waited to hear for a long time.

"Dana, your father called," she said in between puffs.

"Stop playing, Miss Cookie. I know you're feeling good right now but save the hype."

I didn't want to be disrespectful, but I was totally not in the mood to play games. People her age shouldn't be allowed to smoke weed, I thought, as I turned the corner.

"I'm not kidding, Dana."

Her words stopped me in my tracks.

"He called and said he needs to talk to you about something really important. He couldn't give me a number, but he told me to tell you that he loves you and he's hip to what's going on. He said you'd know exactly what he's talking about."

My heart raced and I felt dizzy. He knew. From the moment Mr. James entered my life, this had been my only prayer. Somewhere in the back of my mind, there were still images of my father coming to rescue me. Over time, those images began to fade, and other things eventually replaced them. Where the hell had he been all this time? The transient joy that I felt was quickly replaced by anger, as memories of my first encounter with Mr. James began to play in my head. At that moment, I blamed my father for all of it.

"Yeah, whatever, Miss Cookie. He obviously knows where I am. The ball is in his court."

"Dana, your father loves you. You were too young to understand why he bounced when he did. You need to hear him out," she said.

She was probably right, but I was angry and I couldn't think of any good reason or excuse that my father could use to justify the way things turned out.

"I'm not holding my breath, Miss Cookie. Where was he when I needed him?"

I threw up my hand and left the room.

When I came down from the three lines of coke that I lifted from Mr. James, I fell asleep. Ja'El and I had an early appointment at the nail shop the next morning and it was also time to plan Ja'El's wardrobe for her debut performance. After that, we were gonna head to the club for a quick last minute rehearsal. I didn't have any time to waste on wishful thoughts. Whatever my father had to say wouldn't change what had already happened.

Ja'El already had a few days of practice under her belt and it was clear from day one that she was a natural. Her first night at the club was epic. The fellows loved her. If her first night was any indication, Ja'El would have well over the twenty grand she'd set as her goal for school.

Ja'El and I grew much closer after we started working at the clubs together and I was an official applicant to Gretna State University, the school that Ja'El talked about since we were little kids. Our primary goal was to get out of East Boogie and all of our decisions were made with this in mind. For example, we were doing five am workouts three days a week in order to maintain our moneymaking assets. We figured if push came to shove and we came up on hard times once we left East Boogie, we had options. I was sure we wouldn't be the first college students to earn their tuition on the pole.

The following weekend, Ja'El had an appointment with Miss Henrietta and we were going to do a little shopping afterwards. We finished all of our errands around three and decided to kick it at the park to kill time. Ja'El wasn't in the mood to deal with her family and most likely, Miss Cookie was still in her PJ's at the place that I called "home." I made a conscious effort to give her as much time to herself as possible for fear of becoming an unwelcomed guest. At that moment, I felt the effects of being displaced without a normal home life. Ja'El must have read my mind.

"Dana, this is no way for a child to live. Right now, at this moment, I feel like a motherless child. Why do you think God chose to place us in such a horrible predicament?"

Behind Closed Doors: *Dana's Story*

Ja'El asked the question while she examined the unpleasant scenery around us. Just ahead sat a young lady on the edge of the sidewalk with three little kids. The look of hunger and lack was written on their little faces. On the bench immediately to our left was a middle-aged man, obviously down on his luck. His outward appearance was a dead give-away, but the distinctive smell of abject poverty was the most telling.

"You see the lady with those kids over there, Dana? She was at my house just last night looking to score a couple of rocks from my Uncle Jamar. Where the hell were her kids last night? If I had to guess, I'd say she left them at home alone. This is the type of thing I'm talking about. I look at those kids and I see myself. My mother doesn't give a damn about me and I'm willing to bet you that lady feels the same way about her kids. Have you ever wondered what it would be like to wake up every morning like regular kids and not have to worry about grown folks stuff?"

"I was just thinking along those lines myself, Yah. I don't have a firm answer for you, but I'll try to give you my perspective," I said.

I searched for the simplest way to convey my feelings on the subject.

"It's like this, Ja'El, we can't control where we came from or the circumstances that contributed to our being here, but we can do one or two things. We can wallow in it or we can use it as motivation."

I thought about some of the things my cousin Lenny shared with me a few summers ago when he taught me how to play chess:

"Dana, you can't control most of the things that happen around you. However, you can still control your destiny through your reactions. You have to learn how to adapt and overcome. At some point, you will find that the greatest revenge in life is success. Don't ever forget that, Lil Momma, you heard me?"

After that conversation, I considered telling Lenny about my ordeal, but again, I just couldn't bring myself to do it. At that point, I figured it was all water under the bridge.

"We have a plan, Ja'El. We just gotta roll with it."

Chapter Six
Make It Rain

Miss Cookie usually left the house around five on Saturdays to attend her weekly card party. The parties were held at different homes every week and revolved around a simple game of "pity pat." The weekly event was a potential source of income for the ladies that attended, especially the hostesses. The gig was pretty simple. There were usually five players per table and each player was required to bet a certain amount of money (usually $1 minimum) per each hand dealt. Each hand was worth $4 in total earnings to the winner, and $1 was automatically paid to the hostess. These games were also called "rent parties" for obvious reasons, but the money was also used for things like diapers, lunch money, etc. I'm sure it was used for a few other things as well, like drugs and alcohol. Since Miss Cookie was single with no kids, her earnings were used to maintain her supply of weed, beer, cigarettes, and BC Powder.

Unfortunately, the crack epidemic put a damper on the harmless gambling operation. With the desperation for the drug at an all-time high, "rent parties" were soft targets for individuals on the prowl for quick money. After a few home invasions, the ladies now all carried weapons and had their boyfriends to act as security. A hot mess is the best way to describe it, especially since half the boyfriends were crackheads themselves.

Ja'El and I arrived at Miss Cookie's in time to see her take off with one of her card buddies. We decided to take a nap before we headed over to the Whiz. We alternated weekends between the two clubs in order to avoid becoming too familiar. Since our first set didn't start until almost midnight, we had plenty of time to rest. A loud knock at the door startled me out of my sleep at around nine. Somehow Ja'El slept right through the noise and didn't budge.

"What's up, Dana?"

Mr. James stood at the door with a mischievous look on his face. Why was he even here? He usually met me at the club on Saturdays.

"I was just taking a nap before heading over to the club. What's going on? I thought you were gonna meet me there like always."

I leaned against the doorframe and tried to hide my disgust for this man who was the worst excuse for a human being I'd ever seen. On the other hand, he was also the only person besides Miss Cookie that seemed to care if I had a decent meal or clothes on my back.

"Don't worry, Dana, I'm here for business. You've been acting a little shady lately. If you got some of these snotty nose little boys on your mind, don't even think about it. This stuff belongs to me, and it's up to me if anyone else gets any. Are we clear?"

He stroked my hair with a far-away look in his eyes. The look was gone as soon as it appeared and he was back to business.

"I just wanted to hip you to something that's going down at the club tonight. There's a couple of cats coming in from out of town--some real ballers. I need you and your girl to be on tonight."

We had out of town ballers in the club all the time, so what was different about tonight?

"So, what gives, Mr. James? Is there just one guy you're trying to tag or is it the whole crew?"

I asked because I thought about all of the horrible possibilities associated with this particular scenario and I wanted to know in advance if there was anything to worry about.

"I can't answer that right now. I'll let you know when you get there".

"Just remember, Ja'El isn't down with any of the extra stuff and she wants to keep it that way, Mr. James."

He wouldn't give a rat's ass about my last statement, but I put it out there anyway.

"How 'bout you let Ja'El decide," he said and turned to leave.

"Get there a little earlier tonight. These fellows may be interested in some lap dances before the show and I'm not planning to leave any money on the table tonight."

"Cool," I said and quickly closed the door.

It was close to ten, so I hopped in the shower for a quick shower and shook Ja'El out of her sleep when I finished.

"Ja'El, wake up. We gotta roll out a little earlier tonight. Got some major ballers in town".

That was all she needed to hear. She had her shower cap on over her do-rag before I could get the words out completely. Within minutes, she had her jogging suit on ready to roll.

"Let's be out, Dana."

"Ok, but hold up for a minute. I need to give you the run down on tonight."

"Yeah, I know, Dana. Big ballers, lots of money--I need to make sure and shake my moneymaker real good," Ja'El said with a goofy grin.

She clearly didn't have a clue about the number of things that could potentially transpire that night. The entire situation was a double edge sword. On the one hand, we wanted as much attention as we could get because attention equaled dollars. On the other hand, attention from the wrong kind of guy could lead to serious trouble. Overzealous "fans" had to be handled with care. I looked at Ja'El and concluded she was still green about this sort of thing so I gave her a quick run-down.

"Ja'El, you're right. This isn't brand new. But some of these "baller" guys are lower than snakes. They come in and throw a little money and they think they own you. As you know, some of the girls will do anything for an extra buck. You have to be straight up about what you're willing to do for the money they're spending."

I thought about a chick named Sparkle in particular. With her, anything was fair game and the most it ever got her was a few dollar bills.

"A lap dance is the most you're willing to do. Remember that and make it clear in advance," I warned.

My mind traveled back to my first experience with an aggressive customer. On that particular night, Mr. James decided to dip outside with one of the new dancers. I'd just finished a $500 lap dance for a guy who thought my services included a trip to the back room. He literally tried to drag me into the next room by my hair after I told him I wasn't down with what he suggested. The club was filled to capacity that night, yet no one seemed to notice what was going on in the baller section. When I realized the dude wasn't *taking no for an answer, I panicked and gave him a nice little knee to the groin.*

"I'm kicking your ass, you slimy little..." he growled.

He fell to the floor in a fetal position in mid-sentence. I figured it was a good time to call it quits for the night and decided to head for the nearest exit. Mr. James returned just when I was about to leave the scene.

"What the hell did you do Dana?" Mr. James asked.

I was too outdone with him to give an answer. Why the hell should I have to defend myself 'Mr. I keep my eyes on you at all times?'

"Ask him," I replied. "I'm going home."

"You'll do whatever I tell you to do" he yelled. "You don't run jack-shit up in here. Don't forget that."

"Dana! Don't you hear me talking to you?" Ja'El screamed.

"Yeah, I hear you."

I sighed as Ja'El brought me back to the present.

"Look, stay close to me tonight. Something's up and Mr. James isn't talking. We gotta look out for ourselves."

I was not in the mood to do any favors for any of Mr. James' new "friends" and I was determined to keep Ja'El on the pole and nothing else.

The club usually presented ten girls each night and sometimes more on Saturdays. The girls were split into two groups and rotated on an hourly basis. Ja'El and I were the current main attractions, so Ja'El performed last for the first group and I closed for the second group. While the money was much better at the OZ, I preferred to work at the Whiz because we got to choose our own music. Ja'El was into the old school sounds, and contrary to my prediction, the crowd loved her song selections. The old school players really got a kick out of seeing a pretty young girl dance provocatively to artists like Isaac Hayes, the Bar-kays, and Con-Funk-Shun. Besides that, Ja'El had the pole thing on lock. After the first couple of weeks, she was providing lessons for some of the veterans.

My music selections were more appealing to the younger crowd. My playlist included: *Can He Do It Like This* (Ready For the World), *Don't Wait for Me* (The Time) and *The Beautiful Ones*

(Prince). However, *Darling Nikki* (Prince) was my bread and butter. The lyrics and the sultry interludes in the song provided multiple opportunities for me to "make it rain" with my sensual dancing skills. Ja'El might have had the pole-dancing thing down, but I was the undisputed queen when it came to working my hips on the floor.

As suspected, the club was packed when we got there and we were all seeing dollar signs. My heart pumped extra fast as the adrenaline and excitement kicked into gear. The two lines of coke I snorted before I left the house probably had a little to do with it as well. At any rate, I was ready for whatever and so was Ja'El. She was just as pumped up as I was on her natural juices.

Trina aka Miss Goddess, one of the old heads, was about to get things started when we entered the club.

"Coming to the stage is Miss Goddess," the announcer said, as the Gap Band's *Yearning for Your Love* began to play.

Miss Goddess was probably in her early 30's but her body was like a twenty year-olds. Her boobs were perfect and her belly was as flat as a pancake, with no stretch marks. People around town sort of hated on her because they couldn't understand how she managed to keep her body so tight after having four kids. She was quick to tell them it was her gift from God. Like always, she made it rain effortlessly, and gave the rest of us a very hard act to follow.

After we took a moment to watch Miss Goddess' show, Ja'El and I headed to the dressing room to make our transformations. We had the process down to a science by now, and within minutes we were in our new gear, hair whipped and make-up flawless. By the time we finished, it was Ja'El's turn. She decided to go with one of the crowd favorites, *Voyage to Atlantis* (The Isley Brothers), for her first performance. Her performance to this song was always a crowd pleaser. It was a perfect display of art in motion. She started her routine with a crucifix climb to the top of the pole. Her spinning descent to the bottom of the pole was perfectly timed to coincide with the beginning of the first verse. From there, she incorporated a total of twenty-six pole movements and managed to stay on the pole for almost the entire length of the song (4 minutes 31 seconds), which was a club record. She ended the routine with a Martini spin and a pin-up girl pose. Her performance was off the chain.

Behind Closed Doors: *Dana's Story*

After a brief intermission, the second group of ladies began to take the stage. I got a little nervous when my turn quickly came around. I decided to go with one of my favorite songs...*Do Me Baby* (Prince) to get things started. I came out in a black leather trench coat, red patent leather stilettos, and Ray Bans. Underneath, I wore a new red string bikini and my hair was hidden beneath a cute wide brimmed fedora I'd picked up a few weeks back. As the music began to play, I methodically removed the sunglasses and the trench coat. My hair was the most exotic thing on my body and I used it to my advantage. Posing in a provocative kneeling position with my head bowed, I finally removed the hat to reveal the long wavy mane I'd acquired from my mother. I threw my head back in a sensual manner and allowed each strand of hair to do its own thing. After the dramatic interlude, I began my floor routine with a few seductive body waves, backward wiggles, v-toes and hip circles. After that, I climbed the pole and gave them the business. The crowd was absolutely wild. I didn't just make it rain--I created a tsunami. As I reached the end of my routine, I looked into the audience for the first time, directly into the eyes of the most beautiful thing I'd ever seen in my life. He was a chocolate brother dressed in all black and his bald head glistened under the dim lights. His look was complete with a goat-tee, perfect white teeth, and a chiseled face. He had to be one of the out of town ballers, because nothing about him said East Boogie.

While the crowd continued to applaud, I gathered my things and briefly willed my eyes away from the stranger just long enough to collect the large array of money from the stage. In spite of my preoccupation with the stranger, I noticed there were only a few dollar bills mixed in with the 20's, 50's and 100s. This was just my first dance. If the rest of the night was like this, I was well on my way to a small fortune. When I looked up, he was gone. I searched every inch of the club before I left the stage but he was nowhere to be found. As a matter of fact, I didn't see him for the rest of the night, but I felt his presence. Each time I went on the stage, I performed especially for him and each performance was better than the previous one.

"Dana, what the hell has gotten into you? You're killing it tonight," Ja'El said.

She bounced around the room in excitement and gave me dap. She was more excited than I was at the amount of money I'd collected so far.

"Ja'El, I think I just saw my future husband. I swear, this guy is absolutely gorgeous. But he disappeared after my first dance and I haven't seen him since," I said.

I looked around frantically to locate the stranger.

"Well damn, Dana, where the hell is he? Why didn't you step to him? And why the hell haven't I seen him?"

"Good question," I said and began to panic at the thought to not see him again.

Maybe he was an illusion, I thought, while I dipped into the bathroom for another line of coke.

By then, it was time for our last stage dance, which was a group collaboration. It was an opportunity for the ladies to put our talents on display with a little friendly competition. It was also time for the real ballers to make their selections for the lap dance segment of the show, which was the grand finale of the evening. The DJ customarily selected the last song and it was always a butt-shaker. True to form, the tune for the night was *White Horse* by a group called Laid Back. It was an old tune, but it was an all-time favorite at the Whiz and one of my favorites as well. I immediately made a beeline for the center pole and prepared to go out with a bang. My future husband might be hiding from me, but I wasn't hiding from him. The way I saw it, it was my last opportunity to get his attention and that's exactly what I intended to do. I let the crowd have it once again, but in reality, I danced for one person. I was completely drained by the end of the song and I had a line full of fellows waiting for personal attention. Unfortunately, the person I wanted to see was nowhere to be found. Thoroughly disappointed, I excused myself to the ladies room for a moment, but I already planned to bounce. I didn't care about the money I left behind. I was consumed with thoughts of the chocolate stranger.

Who was he and where the hell did he go?

Chapter Seven
Tyree

I grabbed Ja'El and we hitched a ride back home with one of the other dancers.

"Dana, are you sure you're ready to leave? There's some serious money in there tonight; we could have doubled our money on the lap dances."

"I know. I'm just not feeling it tonight."

"It's all good; I'm kind of tired too. I think I made over two grand, so I'm good. What's up with this dude you're sweating? A few of the other girls were talking about him too. They say he's fine as hell, but where did he go? I'm tripping because I didn't get to see what all the fuss is about."

"I don't know where he went. Maybe he was with Mr. James. His was missing in action all freaking night. I ain't about to tell him I made off with close to 5 G's. He should have been on his j-o-b."

On a night like that, Mr. James would have been posted up at the backstage door, waiting to count my loot. After the first set, I waited until the dressing room was clear and I separated the ones, fives and tens from the larger bills. If he came to see how much I had, I planned to give him the stack of smaller bills.

"You gotta be kidding me, Dana. You made five grand? No wonder your ass was ready to bounce."

"Here, count it," I told her once we were back at Miss Cookie's.

Ja'El would crash with me since it was so late. On top of that, she wasn't down for the Saturday night chaos that was probably taking place at her crib. It was after 3 a.m. and the crack heads were at the peak of their incessant quest for that next hit. Ja'El's loot mysteriously came up missing a couple of times and she was now stashing her money with mine at Miss Cookie's crib.

"Dude, it really is 5 G's," she said after she finished counting. "Is this the most you ever made in one night?"

"As a matter of fact, it is," I said and made my way to the bathroom for a shower.

Behind Closed Doors: *Dana's Story*

I had to get the smell of the club out of my hair before I went to bed or I wouldn't get any sleep.

Ja'El was fast asleep when I returned. I grabbed my pillow and crashed on the opposite end of the bed, which was our normal sleeping position. It was well after noon the next day when Miss Cookie started to bang on the bedroom door.

"Dana, wake up. There's someone here to see you," she said at the top of her voice.

At first I thought it was Mellow, a guy from my homeroom class. His only aspiration in life was to become East Boogie's next kingpin, but his short-term goal was to make me his wife. Mellow was probably the cutest guy in the whole school, however, he was high yellow and that was a real deal breaker for me. On top of that, he was three inches shorter than me and his maturity level was infantile compared to mine. The scenario was laughable at best, but I decided not to hurt his feelings by telling him what I really thought. He was the only brother in the neighborhood with enough balls to step to me, so I let him make it based on this fact alone.

When I finally made it to the hallway, Miss Cookie was waiting for me with a big smile on her face.

"Girl, I need you to talk fast. Who is that tall glass of chocolate milk standing on my porch and where the hell is his daddy?"

She was almost completely out of breath with excitement.

"Miss Cookie, how would I know who's out there? I haven't been out there yet."

I rubbed my eyes and yawned while I made my way to the door. I almost fainted when I saw my future husband standing there with a toothpick in his mouth and a Chicago White Socks cap pulled down to his eyebrows.

"Hello Dana," he said, with a crooked smile.

"Um, how do you know my name?"

I responded in a squeak before I cleared my throat and accepted the stranger's handshake.

"I'll answer all of your questions, if you allow me to take you out to lunch."

He looked at Miss Cookie for permission. She nodded her approval and gave him a big smile before she retreated to her room.

Behind Closed Doors: *Dana's Story*

If it had been anyone else, I probably would have shot him down. Not this one.

"What time would you like to go?"

I asked nervously and wondered what would happen if I ran into Mr. James. How would he react? And how would I explain his reaction to this man? It was enough to make me change my mind about going at all, but, either he was a mind reader or I was doing a horrible job at concealing my apprehension. His next comment was music to my ears.

"No worries, Dana, I got you. You're safe with me. By the way, I'm Tyree Carter. My friends call me Ty."

It was already one and he wanted to pick me up at three. After I finished running everything down to Ja'El, it was almost two.

"Look, I gotta get dressed. I don't have anything else to tell you--for now," I said and made a dash for the bathroom.

I didn't have a clue about what I was going to wear, but I would figure it out while I was in the shower. I was in a daze. Could this really be happening? How the hell did he know where to find me? And why didn't he say something to me last night?

At 2:30, I'd changed outfits for the fifth time. I realized I was lost when it came to normal relationship things--like dating someone who wasn't old enough to be my father and how to dress for a real date. In the end, I decided to go with the first outfit. It was a white off-the-shoulder baby-doll dress that stopped about mid-thigh and some cute brown leather sandals. I pulled my hair back into a long fluffy ponytail and threw on my favorite pair of bamboo earrings. I decided to go light on the makeup, opting for a little eyeliner and pink lip-gloss. I figured less was better since he'd already seen my glamorous side. At precisely 3:00, I heard the knock at the door. My heart started to race and I broke out in a cold sweat. I had to get a grip or I would to make a complete fool of myself for sure.

"Dana!" Miss Cookie yelled. "Your company is here!"

Ja'El nearly knocked me down as she rushed to the living room to see if I was hallucinating about Ty's good looks or if my description was accurate. She did a U-turn after she said hi and walked back into the room.

"Damn Dana, you were right. He's fly AND he got loot. That's what's up," she said, barely able to contain her excitement.

When I entered the living room, Tyree was seated comfortably on the love seat beside Miss Cookie, who fired off questions like a detective.

"Now where you say you from? What brings you to East Boogie?"

"I'm from Markham, Illinois--just outside of Chi-town. I have a few friends down this way. Thought I'd pay'em a visit."

"Is that right?"

Miss Cookie sounded a little skeptical. The drive from Chicago to East St Louis was about four hours long, which was definitely outside of "just dropping by" distance. I prayed that she wouldn't say anything to embarrass me. Thankfully, she kept her thoughts to herself.

"Well, where y'all going? Not many places to choose from around here and most of the decent spots won't open till five o'clock."

"So, I've been told. I was thinking about heading across the bridge to see what's popping on the loop," he said smoothly.

Great choice. Delmar Loop was one of my favorite spots. There were tons of restaurants and boutiques.

"I know Dana has school tomorrow, but I think we can make the trip and have her back at a decent hour."

I was relieved to hear that. At least I didn't have to worry about running into Mr. James.

"Sounds good. Y'all have fun and bring me something good from one of those fancy restaurants," Miss Cookie said.

"Yeah, bring me something too," Ja'El chimed in from around the corner.

Before I could respond, Tyree agreed to their demands and we headed out the door. There was only one car parked out front. One look at the black corvette with the peanut butter top, and I knew Tyree was a baller.

"Nice car," I said when he opened the door for me.

"Thanks."

He put the car in drive and burned rubber as we headed toward the bridge. We rode in silence for a moment and I forgot all about being nervous because I was too busy trying to figure out the name of the artist and the song that came from the Bose speakers. It was a sound I'd never heard before, but I was really into it. When I couldn't come up with a name for the song or the artist, I finally broke the silence.

"Who's that you're listening to?"

"New cat out of Chicago named Robert. Remember, you heard him first right here--the future king of R&B," he said with a grin. "This dude is about to blow up."

"You know him personally?"

"I suppose you could say that. So what you got taste for, little lady?"

For some reason, he quickly changed the subject.

"Nothing in particular; I'm game for whatever," I said.

Truth be told, I was so hungry, I didn't care if we had tuna sandwiches. Thankfully the music was loud enough to conceal the angry sounds that rudely escaped from my belly.

"In that case, I'll take you to my favorite spot--Marty's. It's over in Soulard. Ever been there before?"

"Yes. I love it. They have the best shrimp étouffée I've ever tasted outside of New Orleans. The dessert isn't the greatest though."

"It's all good. The Bread Company is right next door. We can grab dessert there."

The St Louis Bread Company was one of my favorite spots. The cinnamon and brown sugar bagels were the bomb.

He kept the conversation light during our trip across the bridge. Once we were seated at the restaurant, the floodgates opened.

"Dana, what's a beautiful girl like you doing in a place like the Whiz?"

The question threw me off guard.

"I don't really know if I can answer that."

"You mean you can't or you won't."

"Um, I really don't want to talk about it," I said self-consciously.

I felt uncomfortable at the thought of any disclosure of the horrible details of my life to a stranger. If I told him the truth, I probably wouldn't see him again. If I lied, he was bound to find out, I thought, and looked down at the table. The tears came and as much as I didn't want to make a scene, I couldn't stop them.

"Dana, it's okay. I know everything. I know all about your mother and the little arrangement she has with Mr. James."

"But, how..."

"Your father--he sent me here to see if what he heard is true."

"My father sent you here?"

"Yes, Dana. I can't tell you everything right now, but here's the bottom line. Mr. James has been put on notice. If he comes near you again, he's a dead man."

I lost it. Thankfully we were in a booth. Tyree slid in beside me and turned my face into his chest and told the waitress to come back later for our order. I cried like a baby.

"But my mother...."

"...Is a cold-hearted bitch," he finished my sentence. "She isn't fit to be called a mother."

"What's gonna happen now?"

"You'll stay with Miss Cookie and finish school. That's all you have to do. It's what your father wants."

"What about the kids? Mr. James threatened me with my sisters, always saying how beautiful they are. I'm afraid he'll go after them."

"Like I said, Dana, he's been warned. The warning is good for your sisters as well."

"Where's my father? Why didn't he come back for us?"

I asked the question in frustration. Tyree was obviously withholding information about my father.

"It's a long story, Dana. I think you've had enough mental stimulation for the night. Let's just try to enjoy the rest of the evening."

"Okay," I said, unable to hide my disappointment.

I resigned myself to the fact that he'd told me everything he was going to tell me.

We finished our meals and went next door to the Bread Company for dessert. From there we ventured into one of the little coffee shops on Delmar and found a crowd of people watching a grueling game of chess between two former national champs. For a moment, I think Tyree forgot I was even there as he mentally strategized with the players. The crowd went wild when the underdog in the match proceeded to force his opponent into the checkmate position.

Chapter Eight
Karma

The ride back to Miss Cookie's went by pretty quickly. Tyree walked me to the door and asked me to get Miss Cookie.

"Good night, Dana."

"Good night, Tyree."

I wanted to leave a crack in the door, so that I could hear their conversation, but I was too tired to even bother. When Miss Cookie came back in the house, she had a serious look on her face.

"Dana, your friend just told me everything. He even tried to offer me money for letting you stay here. I guess he thought I knew about Mr. James, but God as my witness, I didn't know. I feel like going over there and putting my hands on your momma. How could she do such a thing? Why didn't you tell me, Dana? I feel horrible because I knew something wasn't right years ago. When did he start messin' with you?"

"When I was 12," I said quietly and proceeded to tell her the whole story.

Miss Cookie had to sit down. She was shocked.

"To be honest, Miss Cookie, I thought you were getting a cut from my mom or Mr. James, so I didn't see any point in bringing it up."

"Dana, this is the sickest thing I've ever heard in my entire life. James with his slick talking, slew-footed ass, walking round here like he all that and foolin' round with little girls. I got a notion to turn him in, but Tyree told me not to do it. Your father is taking care of it. As for your momma, I don't know what to say. You think you know a person and then you find out something like this", she said and shook her head.

"Go on to bed, Dana. You got school tomorrow."

"You okay, Miss Cookie?"

She was visibly shaken by the recent turn of events.

"No I'm not, Dana. I'm mad as hell, but I'll be okay in a minute."

She reached under the coffee table and retrieved the cigar box which contained her stash of weed. I went to my room and put on my pajamas. I went to sleep without crying for the first time in years.

The next day, Ja'El was ready to go as soon as I knocked on the door. This was a first. Ja'El was always late, but today was different. She wanted the scoop on my date with Tyree.

"Ja'El, I'm in love."

"Word?"

Ja'El screamed in delight.

"Come on, tell me what happened."

"Nothing happened. We had dinner, dessert, and watched a chess match. After that, he brought me home."

"That's it?"

She looked thoroughly disappointed about the lack of excitement in my date with Tyree.

"Yep, that's it. Not very exciting but he gave me some valuable information. Turns out, my father sent him. Someone must have told him what was going on with my mom and the arrangement she had with Mr. James. Tyree came to put an end to it. It's over, Yah. I never have to see Mr. James again."

"Wow, Dana. I told you to lighten up on your pops. I had a feeling he was gonna come through. Where is he? Is he coming back? And what is your mom gonna do now? You were her meal ticket."

"She can eat shit and die for all I care. I just want to make sure that the kids are okay. After what she did to me, I don't know if they're safe."

"Dana, when was the last time you saw your moms?"

"Hell, I don't know. I make it my business not to see her. It's better that way. As long as I can see the kids, I'm good."

Miss Cookie still brought the kids over from time to time. It was usually on Fridays, which was my mother's club night.

"Why, what's up?"

"Word on the street is your moms is a junkie, Dana. She's on that H."

"No way. My mother hates the smell of weed, how the hell does she go from that to shooting heroin? It's probably just a rumor. Besides, she's still doing hair three days a week. You can't be doing hair and shooting heroin."

"I don't know. I'm just telling you what I heard."

So my mom was an alleged dope fiend. Perhaps that was her reason for pimping me out to Mr. James.

Out of all of the different types of addicts I'd seen in East Boogie, heroin addicts were the worst. The physical dependence associated with the substance superseded even the strongest desire to get clean. Being dope sick was extremely unpleasant and most junkies would do anything to avoid it. You could actually smell a dope sick junkie a mile away, which was good, because it gave you time to take another route. I wanted to go by my mother's crib to see if there was any evidence to confirm the rumor, but I decided to wait and talk to my sisters when they came by Miss Cookie's. Perhaps they would be able to give me some insight.

In the meantime, I had other things to consider. Tyree had informed me of my father's wishes. He wanted me to focus on my senior year and to start thinking about colleges. He would be footing the bill for my tuition. Effective immediately, my days at the strip club were over and Ja'El followed suit. I was a little surprised when she gave up the gig, because she was still a few grand away from her target goal. She said she wasn't down with doing it without me. It was all good, though. Between the two of us, we had close to $27,000. It was more than enough to cover a year of out of state fees and expenses for one student. As far as I was concerned, the money was hers. Of course Ja'El was totally against the idea and flat out refused to accept my offer.

"Dana, that's your money--you earned it. I can't let you do this..."

"Consider it a loan, Ja'El. As long as you owe me, I'll never be broke. Just pay me back when you can".

We stashed twenty grand for Ja'El's first year of school, which left us with $3,500 each for rainy days or a new outfit from time to time.

My relationship with Tyree took off after our first date. He dropped by Miss Cookie's the next day and we rode around the city with the top down on his Vet. We just listened to music and talked. He confirmed his occupation, which was obvious, but he said that he had no aspirations to make it a career.

"Music is my life, Dana. I'm only doing this to set myself up in the music industry. I have one artist right now, and he's a sure thing. I'm looking to sign him to a major label any day."

"You really think you can walk away from all of this?"

"Absolutely. When you hate what you do for a living, it's called a job. When you love what you do, it's a completely different story," he said philosophically.

"So, what are your plans for the future, Dana? I know your pops wants you to go to school, but is that what you really wanna do?"

"Absolutely. Ja'El and I were saving our money for out of state fees and tuition. We're going to school in Louisiana--Gretna State University. Have you heard of it?"

"Everyone knows about GSU. World-famed marching band and the most renowned Black college football team in the country. I guess you can say they put Black college football on the map."

"Yep, that's the one. Can't take credit for choosing it though. Ja'El's been talking about it since Jr. high. I figured I'd just roll with her."

"Looks like your money problems are over baby girl. I want you to just chill and focus on your senior year. Think you can do that?"

"I think so. One question though, did my father send you here to be my body guard?"

"Something like that," he said with a chuckle.

"So, how long are you staying?"

"Until I know that you and the kids are safe."

I thought about what Ja'El told me about my mother. If it was true, my little brother and my sisters were probably in trouble. Without the steady flow of income from Mr. James, my mother would be strapped for cash. There was no telling what she was capable of doing if she was dope sick and broke.

"Tyree, I'm worried about the kids. Word on the street is my mother is shooting heroin. Do you know if it's true?"

"That's one of the things I'm here to investigate, Dana."

"Is it true?"

"It's looking that way, shawty," he said, and confirmed Ja'El's claim.

"We have to get the kids out of there, Tyree."

"I'm working on that as we speak. But don't worry. The kids are safe. School is out in a few days and we're taking them to your grandmother in New Orleans. In the meantime, the kids have a full time nanny."

I was relieved by the information, but I was still in shock.

"My mother is a junkie."

I said the words out loud because I was not totally convinced.

"Are you sure, Tyree?"

"Yes, I'm sure. Mr. James is a pedophile with a thriving dope business. He's also the only heroin dealer in town. The guy is a perverted opportunist and he chooses his victims accordingly. From what I hear, your mother dabbled a little bit back in the day, but never took the full plunge into addiction. When your father left, Mr. James sort of re-introduced her to it. Once she was hooked, he put his bid in for you."

"Unbelievable. All of these years, I thought my mother hated me because I didn't look like her. And now you're telling me that she did all of those horrible things because she's a junkie?"

"It certainly looks that way, Dana".

"Unbelievable. Do the kids know?"

"Right now, the kids don't seem to have a clue. She seems to be a very functional addict--or at least she was a functional addict. Without the steady supply from James, I don't know how long it'll last. It's easy to keep this kind of thing a secret as long as you have a steady supply. Up until now, she's been living a junkie's dream thanks to the pervert. He kept her well supplied. But since he no longer has an incentive to keep her straight, I suspect she'll be in the streets like all the other dope fiends."

When we pulled up to Miss Cookie's house, I saw my mother coming down the street. It was the middle of spring but she shivered as if we were in the dead of winter. Her clothing and hair was a mess. In spite of the excessive number of tattoos up and down her frail arms, the fresh needle marks were very visible. She had all of the tell-tale signs, to include the ugly scabs from the uncontrollable itching and constant scratching. These were common side effects of habitual heroin use. She was obviously in the process of going through withdrawal because the sweat poured profusely from her forehead and she held her belly like she was in severe pain. All of Tyree's predictions became true in an instant. My mother was barely even thirty-five years old and she looked every bit of fifty. I got out of the car and walked toward her. It was close to six months since I last saw her and she looked totally different. After only a day or two without a sufficient supply of heroin, she was already on a downward spiral.

"Dana, who's your friend?"

She gazed at Tyree and saw a potential means to her end. Her words were slow and slurred.

"Tyree, this is my mother. Momma, this is Tyree. Why are you out here like this? And, where are the kids?"

"Oh, they're at home with the nanny. Your father must have hit it big somewhere," she boasted.

"He sent this big fat Haitian chick down here to help me with the kids. Imagine that....me with my very own nanny."

She smiled for no apparent reason. I didn't see a damn thing funny. At that moment, I decided to trash the remainder of the coke that was tucked away in the closet at Miss Cookie's. I was officially scared straight after I saw my mother's condition.

Miss Cookie came out of the house with one hand over her mouth and the other one over her heart.

"Diana, please tell me you ain't back on that shit."

Tyree was right. If my mother was able to hide her addiction from Cookie, she must have been an extremely functional addict and Mr. James must have shelled out tons of dope to keep my mother in line. He gave my mother the worst type of habit known to man and he was generous enough to maintain it. But those days were over. My mother was in serious trouble.

"Cookie, don't come at me with none of that high and mighty bull shit. What the hell does it look like? I'm okay. I just need a little something to get me straight, that's all."

She spoke softly while she scratched and dug her fingernails into her skin as if invisible bugs were embedded in her skin.

"I'm going down to that methadone clinic first thing in the morning."

I knew she was lying, but I didn't say anything.

"I kicked it before and I can do it again. I just need a little something to take the edge off until I can get down there."

The clinic she referred to hadn't been open in years.

"Momma, that clinic doesn't exist anymore," I reminded her. "Why don't you check yourself into rehab? They have one across the bridge. It's open twenty-four hours. Let us take you over there now."

"Look, you little hussy, mind your own god-damn business! You're the reason I'm in the shape I'm in now. If you would have kept your mouth shut, your father never would have found out."

She had it all wrong. I never told my father anything. I could tell she wanted to take her words back because in essence, it was a confession to everything she'd done. Her last statement was about as much as I could stand. I ran in the house with Tyree right behind me. Before I could get inside, I heard my mother scream.

"Come back here, Dana. I need some god-damn money!"

"Diana how could you...?" Miss Cookie asked.

"Oh, shut the hell up, Cookie," my mother interrupted angrily.

"You ain't no better than me. You're probably one blunt away from getting back on the horse. Once a junkie, always a junkie. Don't ever forget that."

After going off on Miss Cookie, she took off down the street toward one of the trap houses.

"Tyree, you gotta do something. I think she's going to the trap house. There's no telling what's gonna happen to her over there."

"Dana, go in the house and try to get some rest. I'll take care of it," Tyree said.

I followed his instructions and stepped into the house, but I didn't think I would get any rest.

"Miss Cookie, can you please tell me what the hell is going on? Did you know my mother was a freaking junkie?"

"Dana, sit down. No, I didn't and I don't know how she managed to keep it from me. Your mom and I became friends when she and your father first moved here. She was already shooting up when I met her and I dabbled a little too, but it was just every once in a while. This is the worst place in the world for a person with an addictive personality like your momma. The monkey was on her back good and tight within a few months and we started getting high together on the regular. Your father was freaking out because he didn't know how to stop her. He finally threw her birth control pills away and got her pregnant, because he thought the pregnancy would force her to quit. He was wrong. She miscarried the baby and they were both devastated. She eventually got pregnant again, with you, and this time she was determined to really quit using. I made up my mind to quit as well, so we did it together. They say it takes three months to form a habit and at least three months to break a habit. I can say for a fact that it's true. After I got clean, I swore I would never use that shit again and I meant it. I suppose that's the reason I've always been so fond of you. You literally saved my life. That's also the reason I never quite understood your mother's indifference to you. And the way she treated your father.....? Well, let's just say she was a damn fool."

"This is just too much, Miss Cookie. What's gonna happen to her now? Having a kid isn't an option this time."

"I can't call it, Dana. I don't know what's going to happen," she said quietly.

"Let me know if Tyree comes back."

I turned away because I didn't want to hear anymore. I went to my room, laid across the bed, and waited. I also cried for my mother.

At around 1:30 am, I heard Tyree's car outside and I ran to the front door. I guess he saw the lights come on because he stayed in the car and waited for me to come out.

"So, what happened? Is she okay?"

"Dana, your mom has one of the worst issues I've ever seen. I finally came up on a bundle of ten bags to get her straight for now. From what she told me, she's doing about two bundles a day, which is damn near twenty bags. That's a lot of dope, Dana. The problem I see down here is that they're pushing low-grade heroin. These greedy bastards are cutting it at least ten times before it hits the streets. Junkies gotta cop a whole lotta dope just to stay straight.

Your boy James is making a killing with that watered down stuff he's pushing."

"Can you break that down for me Tyree? In dollars and cents? I'm totally lost right now. And James in NOT my boy," I said with a little attitude.

"Sorry, Dee, my bad. Not a good choice of words. I just assumed you knew the deal. He is the biggest heroin dealer in town."

"So, I heard. But just for the record, he didn't share that type of information with me."

"Cool. Here's your first lesson in the economics of addiction and distribution. A kilo of pure uncut heroin straight from the Colombians costs about fifty or sixty G's. If you cut it or dilute it to about fifty percent, you can double your ends. Fifty percent purity is pretty common up in Chi-town and that's what the junkies want because you get more bang for your buck. You burn 'em with anything less than fifty percent and lose your clientele. The shit they're pushing down here is probably less than ten percent pure and that's being generous. Since James is the only show in town, the junkies don't have a choice. Here's an example: a bag-a-day junkie in the Chi would have to use at least five bags-a-day down here just to keep from getting dope sick."

"Wow. So, if my mom lived in Chicago, she would only need ten bags-a-day instead of twenty?"

"Close enough. I think you get the picture. Keep in mind we're dealing with street chemists, so the actual purity is never exact. That's why every shot of H has the potential to be your last. Your mom needs help--like yesterday."

"So, what's she gonna do?"

"I don't know. She's talking about rehab, but I don't think she's ready."

"Does my father know about this?"

"He had a strong suspicion, but his hands are tied. I wasn't gonna tell you all of this right now, but I don't have a choice under the circumstances. Your father is in the middle of a fifteen-year bid for trafficking coke. Your mother and Mr. James put him there."

"Come on, Tyree, you gotta be kidding me. You mean he's been in the joint since he left?"

"Pretty much."

"Okay, I'm confused. How do you know my father?"

"I met him on my way out of the joint. We got real cool, real quick. I gotta tell you Dana, the pictures he showed me don't do you any justice", he said.

I wanted to know how my father got the photos, but I didn't want to interrupt Tyree's train of thought.

"He was worried about you coming up in the hood, and from the looks of it, he had good reason. He got in touch with me a few weeks ago and asked me to come down here and check things out. Apparently someone gave him the 411 on what was going down."

"Miss Cookie," I said.

I thought back to the conversation that we had about my father. She told me not to judge him because I didn't have all of the details. It had to be her.

"She stepped to me a few weeks ago about my father."

"Miss Cookie might have given him some information, but she was in the dark about most of it. Someone else gave him the full story. That's what's up, Dana. You're up to speed on everything."

"Where is he?"

"He's in federal prison in El Paso, Texas. I'll give you the contact information later, Dana. It's late, and you need to get some rest."

"Yes, but I need to know how they took him down..."

"They set him up. Your mom knew some of the ins and outs of your father's operation. When he told her that he was ready to get out of the game, she decided to teach him a lesson. She tipped the cops off about a large shipment coming in from Florida and they grabbed him as soon it hit the ground. The really cold part about it was that Mr. James and his crooked cop friends took over half the shipment and flipped it."

"So basically, they stole my father's dope and sent him to jail at the same time."

"Pretty much."

Chapter Nine
Joy and Pain

I fell in love with Tyree that night. He just had a way of making everything seem better. With my mom and Mr. James permanently removed from my life, I was at a crossroad. I could try to live a "normal" life for once or I could hook up with Tyree and stay on the dark path that I had been forced to travel. For as long as I could remember, my entire life had evolved around money. Before my father left, money was never an issue. After he left, there was never enough. It was still hard for me to think about the numerous times that I went to bed hungry and wore hand-me-downs to school after my father left. My mother systematically instilled the fear of poverty within me, which resulted in my insatiable fascination with money. And then she forced me to earn it the old fashioned way. I couldn't see myself living that way again. In the end, I chose the path that would lead me to the good life--or what I thought was the good life. I chose a drug dealer. It wasn't the smartest decision, but I could honestly say it was a conscientious decision--I knew the risks. My decision was based on the fact that Tyree wasn't a typical drug dealer and this was not his long term goal. He was in the game because it provided the resources that he needed to pursue his real dream, which was music. According to Tyree, he was closer than he'd ever been. In the meantime, the stability and profitability of the drug industry was a vital part of the equation.

"I'm telling you Dana, this dude is about to blow up and when he does, I'm leaving these streets behind me."

After I compiled the comprehensive list of reasons to justify my decision to hook up with Tyree, he proceeded to give me a real taste of the good life. Everything I ever wanted was at my fingertips and I didn't have to ask. It was like a real life fantasy tale and my best friend reaped the residual benefits of my good fortune. We were still the flyest chicks on campus because I refused to have it any other way. The feeling I got each morning when Ja'El and I rolled up to the school in the convertible Corvette was indescribable. In spite of the attention, I was so in love with Tyree that I didn't have time to entertain any of it. Overnight, he became my world.

Behind Closed Doors: *Dana's Story*

A month into my senior year, I found out I was pregnant with my second child. My first instinct was to ditch college and continue to enjoy the good life in East Boogie, with Tyree. Who needed college when I had access to more money than I ever could have imagined? My mother was too stoned to care one way or the other.

"I knew you were gonna end up wit' a baby in your belly with all that running around and carrying on you were doing...like you a grown-ass woman."

Did she forget the fact that she forced me into womanhood when I was still just a baby myself? The nerve of this woman.

"Yo baby, yo responsibility. No sense in wasting no money going to college now. You're not smart enough to finish anyway."

However, my grandmother wasn't having it.

"Bring that baby down here to me so you can go on to school," she said.

Even though she'd already assumed guardianship over my brother and sisters, she was determined to take responsibility for my child as well.

"Granny, you're not getting any younger and you have your hands full already," I said to try to reason with her.

"You're going to school Dana and I don't wanna hear anything else about it."

Tyree was excited about the baby and started calling him "Little Ty" before we even found out it was a boy.

"I'm going to give him the world Dana. He will never know what it's like to live in the projects, I promise."

Miss Cookie was a Godsend. She made sure that I had a decent meal every day, did my laundry and tried to fight my battles for me when folks in the community started talking down on me. A pregnant teenager with a junkie for a mother and a father in jail was nothing new in East Boogie. But over the years, my mother had created a few enemies with her superiority complex. Since I was an extension of her, I became the main target and a source of vindication for them. Miss Cookie took up the slack for me since my mom was now living the life of a full fledge junkie. In spite of her being the cause of every hurtful thing that ever happened to me, it still broke my heart to see her that way.

Reality set in when the kids found her on the bathroom floor as a result of another near overdose. The paramedics were there by the time Miss Cookie and I arrived. They took one look at her and administered a dose of Narcan, which is the reversal agent for heroin overdose. The kids were huddled together in a corner and silently took everything in with frightened eyes, while the nanny hovered over them for protection. I could tell she was fed up with the whole scene.

"Dana, your mother is possessed," the Haitian lady said, speaking patois.

I'd heard about voodoo and hoodoo my whole life, but I never experienced it or understood it. Miss Angélique was gracious enough to give me a quick lesson.

According to her, Louisiana voodoo, Haitian voodoo and South American hoodoo are often used interchangeably, but there are distinct differences between the three. Haitian voodoo is a combination of religious customs that were adopted from West African and Roman Catholic beliefs. Images of Catholic saints are often used to represent the "spirits", and the recitation of the Hail Mary and The Lord's Prayer are incorporated in their rituals.

Louisiana voodoo is also a derivative of West African religious tradition, but emphasis is placed on the use of human-like figures and tangible items such as the voodoo doll. Voodoo queens also play an important role in the ritualistic practices of Louisiana voodoo, and the use of occult paraphernalia and snakes are prevalent as well.

While the practice of hoodoo is strongly influenced by both types of voodoo, believers tend to embrace magical or supernatural powers and superstition. Hoodoo herbalism or "root working" is considered a cure-all among believers and often requires the use of an individual's personal possessions or body fluids, such as menstrual blood or urine and hair. Hoodoo is most often used to reverse adverse circumstances such as illness or bad luck, but the other end of the spectrum is totally different. Hoodoo is also used as a tool of destruction to create evil or harm for select individuals.

"Someone put a root on your mother, Dana," Miss Angélique said, "and I'm sorry to tell you, it's the worst I've ever seen."

"But who would do such a thing, Miss Angélique?"

I hung on to her every word and tried to narrow the list of potential suspects.

Based on the detailed description of the three mysterious practices, Miss Angélique was convinced that my mother must have been "hoodooed". I wasn't sure if I could accept anything she said as factual information, but it would certainly explain a lot.

"We may never know the answer to that question, Dana. It had to be someone very, very close to her."

She wandered into deep thought, and then looked at me with glittering eyes.

"Please remember, you must always keep your enemies close and your friends closer."

Tyree and I decided to take the kids to my grandmother in New Orleans earlier than originally planned. They were traumatized from watching our mother fall deeper and deeper into addiction. At first, I thought they might give me some resistance about leaving, but there was none. They were more than ready to go.

Little Ty was strategically positioned on my bladder, effectively turning the eight-hour drive down south into a ten hour drive due to the frequent bathroom stops. The ride was almost unbearable due to my condition, but the complete silence made it even worse. I was absolutely miserable by the time we reached our destination.

Like always, my grandmother was there to greet us with open arms and to make us believe that everything was okay. No one should ever underestimate the power of love or the resilience of children. The kids were visibly relieved, as my grandmother took each of them one by one and cradled them in her arms. That's when I knew for certain they would be okay.

My father wasn't happy about my pregnancy or anything else that was going on. He had to accept things for the way they were and he did what he could from behind bars to make it better. During one of our frequent phone conversations, he tried to make amends.

"Dana, I failed you and the kids in so many ways. If it takes the rest of my life, I will make it up to you. I never should have allowed your mother to manipulate me into this situation. But I guess love is blind. I've accepted the fact that she never loved me".

"How do you know?"

"For her, it was always about the money, but I should have seen the rest of it coming. Your mother experimented with drugs before I met her and it continued throughout the relationship. For some reason, I thought I could save her. But after what she's done to me, and the God-awful things she's done to you, I'm convinced there is no help for her. It's going to take her to her grave."

"I think you're right. Miss Angélique thinks she's possessed. Nothing matters to her anymore. Momma never left the house without a full face of makeup and a fly outfit. Now, the only thing she cares about is her next fix. I'm dealing with all of this the best I can, but I'm worried about the kids. They're not handling it well at all."

"Children are a blessing and a gift from God. I should have reached out to you sooner, but I let my pride get in the way. I didn't want you to know I was in prison. It was a huge mistake, Dana and one that I will regret for the rest of my life. I've talked to the kids and explained the situation. My goal is to stay in their lives as much as I can. As for your mother, I keep telling them she's sick and that it's going to take some time for her to get better.

"I've been telling them the same thing."

"As for you, Dana, I'm not happy with the way things turned out with you and Tyree. I sent him there to handle business, and it didn't include hooking up with my daughter and getting her pregnant. Just to let you know, Tyree was a marked man when I found out you were carrying his child. However, I realized, my grandson deserves to have his father. Dana, you've got your hands full and it's not gonna be easy, but you have to think about your child. I want you to go to school and I want you to finish. Can you do that for me?"

"Yes, daddy," I said just as the telephone recording chimed in to indicate we'd run out of time on the call.

The rest of the school year went by in a flash. Ja'El and I were still thick as thieves and our plan was to get out of East Boogie as soon as we walked across the stage. Tyree was as generous as ever, and the cash flow seemed to be never-ending. I loved Tyree and I trusted him with my life, but I was stacking as much money as I could. I'd been around the hood long enough to know that I could be yesterday's news with my baby's father. All it takes is a big bootie and a smile. In addition, there was always the possibility of Tyree getting popped with a drug charge or worse. His life could be taken by the streets and I would be left to fend for myself and Little Ty on my own. I was determined to be prepared for whatever hand I was dealt.

It was our last week of school and I was eight months pregnant. The walk across the stage with a big belly was not what I envisioned for my high school graduation, but I was cool with it. We were only a few days away from our big day and I should have been excited. Instead, I woke up that morning with a heavy feeling in my heart. My first instinct was to call my grandmother to see if they were okay. Everything was good with her and the kids, so my mind immediately fell on my parents. I couldn't pick up my phone and contact either of them for obvious reasons, so I decided to write my father a letter during homeroom. I asked Miss Cookie if she'd heard from my mom. Last I heard, she'd hooked up with yet another pseudo hustler from around town. With a habit like hers, there was no telling what she was doing to maintain. Miss Cookie hadn't heard from her, so I just said a prayer and hoped for the best.

As I wobbled to the car and fastened the seatbelt over my belly, I couldn't shake the uneasy feeling that came from the pit of my stomach. When I turned the last corner onto Ja'El's street, I saw the flashing lights and the chaos in front of her house. Her grandmother was seated in the front of the squad car with a dazed look on her face. When she saw me, the tears begin to flow, but she didn't say a word. A police officer headed in our direction, and he almost tackled me when I made a dash toward the house.

"Ma'am, you can't go in there. It's a crime scene!"

"But officer, you don't understand, I'm here to pick up my friend for school. I need to get inside."

I felt light-headed as the seriousness of the situation began to sink in. It was quite obvious to me that something horrible had occurred in Ja'El's house. In my heart, I knew exactly what was going on, but I wouldn't allow myself to accept any of the possibilities. Instead, I focused on the front door of the house and waited for her to emerge so that we could make it to school on time.

"Ma'am, there was only one survivor and she's sitting in that car...."

The rest of his comment was lost in my screams, as I directed my anger toward the officer.

"What the hell are you talking about? My friend is in there getting ready for school! Now, move out of my way so I can go get her!"

I refused to accept what he said. I just wanted Ja'El to walk out of the house and get in the car. That was the last thing I remembered. I woke up in the back seat of the squad car as the paramedics attempted to transfer me to a stretcher. Ja'El's grandmother was still in the same spot.

"Dana, they're gone. Every last one of them are gone", she said sadly.

She stared out of the window and slowly shook her head.

"Ja'El saved my life. She pushed me in the closet and covered me with a basket of dirty clothes. She told me not to come out, no matter what. They killed Jamar and Big Rick first. Arlene was next. And then, they killed my baby. I could hear her scream and beg for her life, but they did it anyway. What did that child ever do to deserve this?"

I was taken to the hospital and admitted for pre-term labor. I gave birth to Little Tyree just hours after I lost my best friend. Miss Cookie and Tyree were there for the delivery. The entire labor and delivery process was a complete blur. I was so doped up, the only thing I remember is the sound of my baby's first cry. He weighed 4 pounds 8 ounces. Although he came a few weeks early, he was the healthiest preemie they'd ever seen, according to the staff. He would remain in the hospital for weight gaining purposes, but other than that, he was perfect. I was released three days after the delivery, which was also the day before Ja'El's funeral. Ja'El's mother and her uncles were laid to rest earlier that day, but I was unable to attend. Miss Cookie filled me in. According to her, it was the saddest thing she'd ever witnessed in her life. To see a mother mourn for all of her children at the same time was just too much. I was glad that I couldn't attend.

Behind Closed Doors: *Dana's Story*

Tyree took me to see Ja'El's grandmother as soon as I left the hospital. She'd moved in with her sister who lived in the same housing project, but in a different building. After she removed her pictures and other personal belongings, she instructed the office manager to burn everything in the old apartment. She planned to move back to Mississippi where the rest of her family remained after the great migration north. According to her, the move to East St Louis was the worse decision she and her husband ever made. When they relocated to the area over fifty years earlier, the city's economy was strong and her family had a good life. After her husband passed away, her home was paid for and his pension was more than enough for her to live on for the rest of her life. However, one by one, she lost all of her children to the streets as crack cocaine permanently destroyed her family. She borrowed against the equity in her property to keep her sons out of jail, but eventually lost the house. She was forced to move into the projects with her daughter and Ja'El. Her sons soon followed suit.

"I should have taken Ja'El and moved back to Mississippi years ago, Dana, but I just kept thinking things would get better. Ja'El was a good child. She wanted to go to college and get me out of here. That's what she told me every day. That night when those hoodlums came to the house, Ja'El knew exactly what was going to happen. She could have slipped out of the window, but she didn't. Instead, she took the time to put me in the closet and cover me up. She told me to stay there no matter what and that's what I did."

"Miss Jamison, there was nothing you could have done; you were no match for them. They came there to do evil and that's what they did. God spared your life for a reason."

"I know, baby. God ain't gon' put no more on me than I can bear. The preacher talked about Job from the bible in his sermon today. You know Job lost everything he had and he still trusted God. I've been hearing that story all my life Dana, and now I'm living it. If I didn't have my faith, I'd have given up a long time ago. It just hurts something awful right now, but this too will pass."

"Miss Jamison, I'm not trying to get in your business or anything, but did you have enough coverage for all of the funerals and the burials?"

"Well, my husband and I had all the kids covered, but I never got around to getting a policy for Ja'El," she said and broke down in tears. She said she had to make payment arrangements for Ja'El and that she was being put away in the cheapest casket they had.

My girl was not going out like that.

"Miss Jamison, don't worry about it. I think we can pull some strings down at the funeral home. Was there anything special you wanted to do, any particular flowers, or anything....?"

"I just wanna put my baby away nicely Dana. She sacrificed her life for me. That's the least I can do and I can't even do that."

"Don't worry, Miss Jamison, it's done."

When we left, I was on a mission and Tyree knew what was up.

"You don't have to say nothing, Dana. I got you. Whatever you wanna do, I got you."

When we made it to the funeral home, Tyree requested someone from management. The girl at the front desk took one look at Tyree's three-finger diamond ring and the Gucci shirt he wore and she summoned the owner.

"I'm here to take care of the funeral expenses for Ja'El Jenkins. There's not a lot of time, since the funeral is tomorrow, but I want the top of the line--from the casket to the flowers and the car you send for her grandmother. Tell 'em what you want, Dana; I gotta step out for a moment."

"Right this way ma'am. Would you like to view the remains?"

"I can't. I'm not ready. Just show me what you have."

I couldn't bear to see Ja'El's lifeless body. The funeral home director took me to the insulated warehouse out back, straight to the premium merchandise. Initially, I planned to choose something pretty and feminine. However, the casket that I selected was the complete opposite. It was black, trimmed in 48-ounce copper and bronze--the highest available grade. I chose black and gold because they were the school colors for Gretna University, the place where Ja'El believed she would find the solutions to all of her problems. Copper and bronze are precious metals, and not only are they beautiful, they are also strong and resilient...just like Ja'El. The

Behind Closed Doors: *Dana's Story*

interior was antique white with softly crushed velvet material, which provided the perfect contrast for the rich exterior accents. I chose it without looking at the price tag because it captured everything about Ja'El. I already had the perfect dress for her to wear. It was the dress she'd chosen to wear underneath her graduation gown. It was hanging in the closet at Miss Cookie's, along with all of her other valuable belongings. By the time Tyree came back, all of my selections were made, with the exception of the flowers. I couldn't make up my mind, so Tyree instructed the directress to use her best judgment. He didn't flinch when the final bill was presented. He simply handed over the cash.

"Thank you, Tyree."

"No need to thank me Dana. Ja'El was your girl. She deserves the best. I gotta make a run across the bridge, but I'll be back for the funeral service tomorrow," he said with a kiss. "I love you Dana."

"I love you too." I was hoping he'd stick around, but I understood. "Be careful."

I couldn't leave Little Ty in the hospital by himself all night, so I stayed with him. The little pullout sofa in the parents' waiting room was hard as a brick. Needless to say, I didn't get much sleep. Thoughts of Ja'El filled my mind and I tossed and turned all night.

I left the hospital in time to get dressed and head to the funeral with Miss Cookie and Tyree. I thought my mother would have had the decency to show up at the funeral, but she was nowhere to be found. The church was packed in true East Boogie fashion. This was typical behavior whenever a young person died. As I walked into the church, my attention immediately fell on the pulpit and I became sick to my stomach. One of Mr. James' "associates" sat in the pulpit with a pompous look on his face. He was one of the men who might have fathered my first child. I rarely ever went to church, so I had no idea that this man was a so-called minister. If this was the kind of man that God would choose to "spread the gospel" and "save the world", we were in serious trouble. I digressed for a moment and allowed myself to contemplate the preacher's reaction if I walked up to the podium and asked him to submit to a paternity test. Those thoughts were quickly replaced by another thought when I considered the fact that a paternity test would be impossible

Behind Closed Doors: *Dana's Story*

to perform in the absence of my son. Inside my purse was a cute little .22 with a pink handle. Tyree insisted that I carry it with me at all times. What would happen if I delivered one of those hollow point bullets right between the preacher's eyes? He nearly fainted when he saw me standing there. Our eyes locked for a few seconds, as I stood in the middle of the church and contemplated murder. I had a good mind to put him on Front Street, but decided against it. It was the wrong time and the wrong place. As I moved further down the aisle, I took note of the other familiar faces scattered around the room, alongside their wives. The overwhelming anger that I I felt was indescribable. Once again, murder was the first thing that entered my mind. Unfortunately, I didn't have enough bullets to fully rectify the matter. As my anger heightened to the point of uncontrollable rage, I was inundated by a sudden sense of calm. At that moment, I knew that each of them would pay dearly for their transgressions...eventually.

When it was finally time for me to review Ja'El's remains, another wave of emotion began to consume my body; this time it was despair. Up until then, I had been forced to keep my emotions in check. I had to be strong for Little Ty. However, the sight of my friend and the finality of the situation nearly brought me to my knees, but Tyree was there to keep me from falling. He stood there with me and allowed me to cry.

"That's it Dana, let it go...you've held it in long enough..." Of course, he was right. I stood there and cried for what seemed like forever and no one objected.

I don't remember walking to my seat. The remainder of the ceremony was like a hazy dream. As we exited the sanctuary behind Ja'El's casket, reality began to set in. The eerie thing about the massive crowd that overfilled the sanctuary and spilled out into the street was the fact that Ja'El's killer could very well have been among the mourners. There were no suspects in the quadruple homicide and since Ja'El's grandmother hadn't seen the culprits, the case could possibly go unsolved. Ja'El's funeral was by far the saddest thing I'd ever experienced in my life and even after I sat through the entire service, it still didn't seem real. When they lowered her casket into the ground, I felt like a piece of me was going with it along with all of our hopes and dreams. In the midst of my overwhelming despair, an all-consuming rage came over me. Someone was going to pay for this.

Chapter Ten
Res ipsa loquitur....It is what it is.

After everything I'd been through in my life, the loss of my best friend had to be the hardest. I suppose everything truly does happen for a reason and nothing ever simply occurs by chance. If I didn't have Little Ty, I honestly don't know if I would have made it. He gave me a reason to go on. He was released from the hospital in time to attend my graduation. He was still a tiny little thing, but he was strong. My grandmother was old school, so she wasn't keen on the idea of Little Ty attending the graduation. "That baby don't need to be around all of those people Dana."

She finally gave in at the last possible moment.

Graduation day was bittersweet. It was supposed to be the day that Ja'El and I would start our new lives. Instead, I had to sit on the stage without her. When Ja'El's grandmother came up to receive her diploma and the award for being the top student, I lost it. Thankfully I was second to last in the processional, so I had time to regain some of my composure.

"Dana Toussaint."

The principal said my name twice before I could move. I turned the corner and looked directly into Tyree's eyes. He was holding Little Ty. It gave me the strength that I needed to take those final steps across the stage.

My father was locked up and my mother was nowhere to be found. It was all good though because my Louisiana family was there to support me. My cousin Lenny even showed up looking as dapper as ever. He was a couple of years ahead of me and about to enter his junior year at Delaney University, an HBCU out in Tennessee.

"Congratulations, shawty! I'm proud of you. Don't forget what I told you...play your cards close and always stay two steps ahead of the game"

"I won't forget, Lenny."

"The fellows are gonna be on you like crazy down there at Gretna. Have fun, but don't forget your purpose. You see that little fellow over there?" he said pointing at Little Ty. "That's your reason for being there."

Behind Closed Doors: *Dana's Story*

My Uncle JP, Jean-Pierre Toussaint, was a special surprise. He flew in from Miami for the ceremony without a word to me of his plans to come.

"I wouldn't have missed this one for the world, baby girl. You are your father's pride and joy," he said with a thick Haitian accent. "He wanted me to let you know that we are here for you and to remind you that you have another family. I should have done this a long time ago, but your mother went out of her way to keep us out of your lives. Here's all of my contact numbers and I want you to call me at least once a week to let me know that you're okay," he said handing me a large white envelope "You are destined for greatness little one, and so is your son. You have Toussaint blood running through your veins."

"Thanks Uncle JP. I wanted to call you so many times..."

"It's okay. It's all behind you now. I want you to focus on your future. When you get to Gretna, you will find that your tuition is already paid for the entire year. You have nothing to worry about except your education. I've spoken with your grandmother and she is determined to keep Little Ty with her even though she has her hands full with your brother and sisters. I want you to know that my wife and I are prepared to take him if we need to. As for your baby's father, I've been checking him out. He's a lot like Bernard. I don't have to tell you anything you don't already know about that. Be careful. Keep your eyes and ears open at all times. Do you understand?"

"Yes".

I read between the lines. My uncle didn't care for Tyree, but it was understandable. He didn't hang around after the graduation. He flew back to Miami right after my celebration dinner. The rest of us spent the night across the bridge in one of the five-star hotels, thanks to Tyree. I couldn't stand the thought of being in East Boogie that night without Ja'El.

The strangest thing happened that night. Maybe it was the words of wisdom that I got from my cousin Lenny and my uncle JP that triggered my suspicion or maybe I was nervous about going away to school and leaving Tyree and Little Ty behind. For the first time, I realized Tyree was as much a mystery to me that day as he was the day that I met him. He never really told me anything about his family and I never asked any questions. Suddenly I was curious. Was he hiding something?

As luck would have it, Tyree left his wallet on the dresser when he went downstairs for a coke and some ice for the Hennessy. Situated neatly behind his driver's license, I found a beautiful family portrait with "The Carters" written at the bottom. Tyree held a little boy, a couple of years older than Little Ty and the female in the picture held a little girl's hand. After the sinking feeling finally subsided and the urge to regurgitate went away, I was hotter than fish grease. Really? Not once, in a whole year, had he mentioned anything about a wife or a family. Did he not think this was vital information? My first instinct was to place the picture on the bed so that he could see it when he returned. But in the end I decided to take my cousin Lenny's advice--life was indeed a game of chess. It wasn't really about the actual circumstances or the situation; my reaction would determine the outcome. When he returned to the room, Little Ty and I were snuggled in the bed.

From then on, my relationship with Tyree consisted of a series of calculated moves and my goal was to stay three steps ahead of him at all times. On the outside, everything was the same. I was the girlfriend, the lover, and the "baby momma" and I acted accordingly. On the inside, I was bitter and angry; but most of all, I felt betrayed. He played me. It was as simple as that. Before I met Tyree, men were simply a means to an end for me, thanks to Mr. James and his foul friends. Tyree had been slick enough to change my mind but his betrayal renewed those feelings and they were stronger than ever. It would never happen again. From that moment forward, my heart was officially off limits.

I spent the summer in New Orleans with my granny and the kids. Dahlia and Dominique were entering their early teens and they seemed to be well adjusted considering everything they'd gone through. Dahlia was the older of the two and at fourteen she was determined to take up the slack in our mother's absence. She looked out for Dominique and Omari like they were her own and she absolutely adored Little Ty. I wasn't completely sold on the idea of leaving my son and going off to college, but Dahlia relieved any remaining apprehension.

"We got this, Dana," she said when I broke down and told her what a hard time I was having to leave Little Ty.

"You have to go to school, Dana. What else are you gonna do? Are you going to hang around and wait for section 8 like momma did when daddy left? You can't go out like that, Dana. I won't let you."

Dahlia clearly had the fierce determination of my father; and somehow, it was unscathed. Her words resonated with me. They gave me the inspiration and motivation that I needed to move forward, but I still had to be sure that I was doing the right thing.

"Dahlia, Granny means well, but she isn't as strong as she used to be. I can't do this without you. You gotta keep your head in the right place or this will never work. Do you understand what I'm saying?"

"Yes, I understand. You're telling me not to get caught up in the streets. Leave the boys alone, that kind of thing. I get it Dee. I'm telling you, I got this."

"There are so many things I wanna say to you Dahlia, but I'm not sure if it's the right time. However, I will tell you this--I didn't choose the streets; the streets chose me. I just played the hand I was dealt."

"You don't have to tell me Dana; I already know," she said. It was all I needed to hear. I wasn't sure if she knew everything, but I was convinced she knew enough.

I was finally at peace with my decision to go to school. However, I still had some other serious issues that needed to be addressed. The situation with Tyree was calm for the moment but it could change at any moment. My plan was to continue the relationship for as long as I could without hipping him to the fact that I knew all about his secret life. The hardest thing about Tyree's betrayal was his ability to make me forget that he was a liar and a cheater. His attentiveness to Little Ty and me was more than I could ever ask for. He was in New Orleans every weekend like clockwork to make sure that we had everything we needed. I couldn't but to wonder how he was able to justify the frequent absences away from his wife and kids. Either she was one of those "blinded by love" type women or she had some extra-marital activities going on as well. I prayed for an opportunity to have a much needed conversation with Mrs. Carter, even though I knew the chances were slim.

My graduation gift turned out to be the biggest surprise of all. Three days before I left for Gretna, a brand new Toyota Celica was delivered to my grandmother's house. The car was black with peanut butter leather interior and fully kitted. In the trunk of the car, was a set of authentic Louis Vuitton luggage and another Dooney and Bourke bag to add to my already robust collection. I stood speechless as my sisters jumped around and screamed. My grandmother came to the porch to investigate the commotion and immediately returned inside. She was clearly disgusted by yet another display of the "evil rewards" that came with "sinful living" as she called it.

Tyree was making it extremely hard for me to write him off completely. I was beginning to think that maybe his love for me was genuine. He wouldn't have been the first man to find himself trapped in a loveless marriage. Unable to contain the information any more, I decided it was time to put all of the cards on the table,

"Tyree, how long have you been married?" I asked, while lying in his arms. It was our final night together before I left for college. I figured now was as good a time as any to have the conversation.

"I was wondering when you would get around to asking that question. Gotta give it to you, Dana, you held out much longer than I expected. In case you didn't know, I'm an extremely observant individual. Nothing gets past me. The night you went through my wallet, you failed to put things back the way you found them. The picture--it was turned the wrong way."

"You're kidding me, right?"

"No Dana, I'm not."

"Wow. So just when were you planning to tell me Tyree--or were you?"

"It's like this Dana. My marital status is only disclosed on a need to know basis--you didn't need to know."

"You bastard..."

"Watch your mouth Dana. You should never bite the hand that feeds you. Didn't your father tell you that?"

"No, he never got around to it," I said trying to get my feelings in check. "Can you just answer my question?"

"How long have I been married? Long enough."

"So, that's all you have to say?"

"It's all you need to know."

Everything was out in the open. Once again, I was the pawn. According to Tyree, he started out with good intentions, but at some point, "things changed," he said.

"Did you get me pregnant on purpose?"

"No, in all honesty, I didn't. I guess you could say Little Ty is collateral damage. The bottom line is this, I have a wife and a family and they aren't going anywhere."

"Really? Well, I just have two questions."

"I'm sure I have two answers."

What about us?"

"You and Little Ty? It is what it is. I'm a man and I take care of my responsibilities, simple as that. What's your other question?"

"Does your wife...?"

"No, she doesn't," he said before I could finish, "and it's in your best interest if she never finds out. So don't get any ideas."

Tyree Montrell Carter was a cold-hearted bastard. I couldn't help but to wonder how many stray kids he had running around besides little Ty. Did he really refer to my son as "collateral damage?"

If this was the game he wanted to play, I was down.

"What's the deal Tyree? What do you want from me? You can't be doing all of this for nothing," I said thinking about the car and all of the other gifts I'd received over the past year. I never asked for any of it, but like the old saying goes--if it seems too good to be true, it probably is.

"Glad you asked. I'm expanding my business further south and I need someone to be the "liaison" between me and my new connection down in Texas."

"So let me get this straight. You want the mother of your child to transport drugs for you? Is that what you're saying?"

"Don't say it like that Dana. First of all, you owe me; or did you forget? I rescued you, remember? Second of all, you won't be doing it for free."

"How much?"

That was my only question after I took a moment to consider his statement. I'm a true product of my environment--money always had a way of piquing my interest.

"Ten G's every time you cross the Texas state line."

It would be more than enough to take care of my family. In addition, a refusal would likely result in Tyree withdrawing his support. My grandmother was on a fixed income with four extra mouths to feed. I suppose my Uncle JP was a potential resource, but he was already paying my tuition. My back was against the wall and from the looks of it, I didn't have very much of a choice. The next morning, Tyree handed me a sheet of paper with the directions and the address to the link up spot in Dallas. At that moment, I recognized the culmination of a well-executed plan. And I actually fell for it.

I decided to spend the morning with Little Ty and the rest of my family. I hit the road around noon, which was much later than I planned. My heart was heavy with fear and anger. In a hidden compartment of my new car, beneath the Louis Vuitton luggage and the twenty-three boxes of shoes were five kilos of cocaine.

According to Tyree, the Mexicans and Columbians ran the show when it came to the cocaine business. In the 80's, a kilo of ninety per cent pure cocaine straight from Bogota Colombia was worth twenty G's, and by the time it was "stepped on" a few times it was worth about sixty G's on the street. After a little quick math, I realized I was sitting on anywhere from sixty thousand per kilo to somewhere around three hundred thousand dollars for 5 kilos.

The main port of entry was Miami and the customary flow was from the bottom to the top and east to west. However, Tyree's operation was a little different. My job was to transport the goods from New Orleans to Dallas and the final destination was somewhere on the east coast. I was curious about the directional change, but decided it was probably best if I knew as little as possible about that part of the operation. To be honest, the only thing that mattered to me was the conversion of kilos to dollars and the number of years I'd have to spend in jail if I was caught. As I listened to Tyree's rant about the ins and outs of the business, the magnitude of the situation became painfully clear.

"What's the maximum sentencing for this kind of weight?"

I still needed to consider the risks versus the benefits.

"Eight to ten fed time."

"That's a lot of time Tyree. I don't know if it's worth the risk."

"Think about it Dana. You're a college student, traveling back and forward to school. If you get stopped, what reason would they have to search your car?"

I thought about it for a moment and decided he was probably right. I figured the chances of me getting pulled over for suspected trafficking were minimal. In the end, I decided it was a chance I was willing to take.

"I'm in."

Chapter Eleven
GSU

My first drop-off went down without a hitch and I had ten G's to add to my stash. My plan was to open a bank account in my little sister's name as soon as possible. If anything ever went down, I figured the money would be untraceable. Tyree's earnings for the transaction would be handled by another female runner. He didn't offer any specific information about her identity and I didn't care enough to ask. However, he did tell me that she was from my hood and that her sole purpose in the operation was to transport money from Dallas to East St Louis. I wondered what she had to do to get that particular position; but once again, I didn't care enough to ask.

During the first leg of my trip, I could think of nothing except the five kilos of cocaine in my trunk and what I would do if I got pulled over. Once the drop was made, my thoughts immediately fell on Ja'El. Before I left East Boogie, I had a long talk with my friend Mellow about the murders.

"Mellow, I have to find out who did this. If you hear anything, let me know."

"For sure Dana. I got you. And just for the record, when you come back, these streets are gonna belong to me--believe that."

"It's all good Mellow, but these streets don't owe me nothing and if I were you, I would get the hell up out of here." I couldn't believe it. After all the bloodshed and tragedy, his ambitions were still the same. What else was it going to take for him to finally get the picture?

After driving around the city for what seemed like forever, I was thoroughly exhausted by the time I spotted the exit that would lead me to Interstate 20. I drove for as long as I could and finally decided it was time to pull over and get some rest. I spent the night in a little east Texas town called Carthage. At first, I wasn't even sure if the little town had a hotel because of the seemingly desolate surroundings. At the last possible moment, I came across a relatively new Best Western about a mile from the exit. It was actually pretty nice and I managed to get some much-needed sleep. I got up the next morning at around 6 a.m. and made a quick stop at the Burger King for some breakfast. As I entered the building, I ran into a young lady wearing a GSU t-shirt. I asked her if she attended the school and she said that she was entering her first semester.

"How cool? So am I. What dorm will you be staying in?" I asked.

"Wheatley Hall."

"So am I. It must be the freshman dorm. What's your major?"

"Pre-nursing."

"Wow, I hear the nursing program at Gretna is pretty tough."

"Yeah, I know, but I'm down for it--can't think of anything else I'd rather do."

"I'm Dana by the way. I'm from East St Louis."

"Cool. I'm Tracy and I'm from right here in good old Carthage, Texas," she said with a little laugh.

After our orders were completed and we both had our food, we talked for a while longer and made our way to the door. Tracy proceeded to tell me how excited she was to leave her little town.

"This is one of the happiest days of my life. I can't wait to get out of here," she said. "The only downside to it is leaving my son. He'll be four next month. I'm planning to move off campus and bring him down to Gretna before he starts kindergarten."

"I have a little one at home as well, so I know how you feel" I said, referring to Little Ty. However, I was thinking about my oldest son, who was actually the same age as Tracy's little boy. I often wondered where he was, or even worse, was he still alive? I wouldn't put anything pass my mother at that point and I wouldn't have been surprised to find out she left him in a dumpster.

"He's with my grandmother in New Orleans, but you just gave me a brilliant idea. I'm gonna see if I can make arrangements for my son to come and live with me."

"We can work on it together," Tracy said. "There's a daycare center about a block away from the campus, but I heard the waiting list is a mile long. I figure if we sign up now, we might have a chance for next fall. It was really nice meeting you Dana. We gotta keep in touch," she said and got into the car with her family.

Her little boy was absolutely adorable. After meeting Tracy, I felt better about my decision to leave Little Ty. I was doing what

Behind Closed Doors: *Dana's Story*

I had to do in order for us to get ahead. I wanted to live a normal life and I wanted to give my son all of the things I never had.

Within minutes, I was headed east on Interstate 20, and the sunrise was beautiful. The thirty-minute drive toward the Louisiana state-line went by pretty fast and then all of a sudden I was just sixty miles away from my destination--Gretna State University. I was on an emotional roller coaster, both nervous and excited about my new life. However, the overwhelming feelings of guilt sort of overshadowed everything. Leaving Little Ty was something I could justify; but for some reason, I was really struggling with the fact that I was actually going to Gretna without Ja'El. I felt like I was living her dream instead of my own. It was a feeling I just couldn't seem to shake. As I turned onto exit 81, I took a deep breath and decided to try and make the best out of a bad situation.

As I drove around the campus in search of my dorm, the excitement began to grow. My heart went into overdrive as I rolled past the area designated for fraternities and sororities. Aside from watching School Daze and episodes of A Different World over and over again with Ja'El, I didn't know much about any of the organizations. From what I could gather, Ja'El was more interested in the uppity, pretty girl group. I really didn't have an interest one way or the other, but I decided to keep an open mind.

I must have driven around the campus two or three times before I finally located my dorm. I received all kinds of looks from the massive groups of people congregated all around, but it didn't take me long to realize all of the attention was due to my new ride. With ninety percent of the students on foot, anyone with a car sort of stood out, especially a sleek looking, shiny, black sports car. I knew right away I would have a hard time making friends with the females, but making friends with the guys wouldn't be a problem at all. After I finally completed all of the registration paperwork for the dorm, I unloaded my car. On the first trip to my room, I met my roommate Alex and I knew we were going to hit it off immediately. She was a very pretty girl and seemed really down-to-earth, but everything about her screamed country. Without hesitation, she volunteered to come downstairs and help me unpack my car.

"Dana, your car is off the chain!" she said when she realized which car was actually mine.

"Thanks, girl. It's my graduation gift."

"Is it a stick shift?"

"Yes," I said as I opened the trunk of the car to reveal the expensive set of luggage and excessive number of shoes and purses. I noticed the inquisitive look on her face and for some reason, I decided to spill my guts right then and there to this complete stranger.

"Okay Alex, here's the deal. All of these gifts were compliments of my boyfriend--the car, the luggage, the shoes, the purses and the clothes."

"Wait a minute. You're telling me some guy bought you all of this stuff just because you're his girlfriend? I don't get it..."

Talking to Alex was easy because she listened without passing judgments. I guess you could say it was therapeutic because the more I talked, I felt like a weight was being lifted. I told her a lot but not nearly as much as I could have told her. By the time I was finished, she knew all about Ja'El's death, Little Ty and my recent discovery about Tyree's marital status.

"Married? You mean to tell me he's married? Girl, you need to write a book. I'm serious," she said, thoroughly outdone with the last bit of information.

I rolled on my bed in laughter because I knew she was serious. I hadn't laughed that much in years it seemed and it felt good.

"Look, let's take a tour of the campus and see what's popping," I suggested, and Alex was game.

Because of all the pedestrian traffic, we decided to walk. Even without the shiny black car, we were still got our share of attention as we made our way to the village. The village was a popular hangout located within walking distance of the campus. In order to get to the village, we had to make the stroll past fraternity row. Alex was thoroughly excited with the scenery on Q-hill, and I finally had to tell her to stop gawking and play it cool. As we got closer, the fellows stopped what they were doing and focused all of their attention on us. We kicked it in the same spot much longer than we intended. We finally accepted an invitation with two of the fellows to an impromptu house party off campus.

Up until then, I had never considered any type of relationship with anyone as close to my age as Dee-dog but there was just something about him. He had game like a well-seasoned player. When we reached the "party" spot, we realized there were only four attendees. Dee led me straight to the bedroom and quickly introduced me to a different type of seduction. The first thing he did was put on some old school music, which seemed completely out of character for his age. He scored major points with that one.

"What's your favorite drink Dana?"

"Hennessy," I said without hesitation.

"Wow. That's a grown woman's drink, Dana, you sure you can handle it?"

"Trust me, I'm a grown woman."

"Well, today is your lucky day for two reasons: I have a little Hennessy and I'm a grown man," he said mixing my drink from the little makeshift bar he had in his bedroom.

From there it was on and popping. When I woke up the next morning, I felt like I'd just completed the Boston marathon and the way Alex was glaring at me, I must have looked like it as well.

It was not the way I planned to spend my first night at Gretna, but that's how it went down. Naturally, I blamed Tyree. What took place that night was a result of his betrayal--I guess you could call it secret revenge. As trifling as it was, my experience with the complete stranger was deeper for me than I anticipated. For the first time, I felt like I was sharing my body because I wanted to, as opposed to doing it because it was required. Sex had always been a symbol of oppression for me; but all of a sudden, I felt free. I didn't have any aspirations for a relationship with Dee because I knew he had a girlfriend. And from our brief and intermittent moments of conversation throughout the night, I suspected he had a few other chicks scattered around campus as well. In spite of the brevity of our encounter, he would always hold a special place in my heart.

After they dropped us off at our dorm, Alex began her interrogation.

"What the hell were y'all doing in there last night?"

"Well, what do you think we were doing, Alex. And what were you and Ken doing last night?"

"We played Super Mario Brothers all night. Ken saved the princess and we went to sleep."

"You gotta be kidding me."

"Nope. He was an absolute gentleman."

"Interesting. Well, let's just say Dee and I got to know each other really well."

"But Dana, what about your boyfriend back home? What's up with that?"

"What about him?" I asked sarcastically. "I'd bet you a pair of my brand new Nike's he was doing the same damn thing last night. Men are good for a few things, Alex, but not many. Until someone proves me wrong, that's what's up."

My experience that night sort of opened the floodgates. Before I knew it, I was a hot commodity on campus, especially with the upperclassmen. I hate to admit it but I became the true definition of a "season girl." During football season, I had a fling with the quarterback and after that, I kicked it with the star of the basketball team. Because of my hefty bank account and steady income, I was able to lead a pretty clandestine life and everything was kept on the low. All of my escapades took place off campus at one of the few hotels in the neighboring town and I made sure that everyone was down with my no strings attached policy. The last thing I needed was a serious relationship.

Things were going well with the little arrangement I had with Tyree. I had successfully completed two trips in the fall and three trips in the spring of my first year at Gretna. It was a total of $50,000 added to the $20,000 Ja'El and I had stashed for her first year. I also had the "rainy day" fund that I started when I first hooked up with Tyree. Those funds were kept readily available and well hidden in my dorm room. As much as I loved beautiful things, I was smart enough not to spend all of my money in Pecanland Mall. Thankfully, all of the major shopping venues were located far enough to prevent me from giving in to the temptation. My monthly expenditures included twelve hundred dollars to Granny for Little Ty and the kids and a few hundred extra for Dahlia and Dominique. Just the thought of my sisters getting pulled into the streets for a pair of sneakers or a new outfit made me physically ill and I stressed my feelings to them on a daily basis.

"Anything y'all need, just ask me. Let those thirsty negroes know that you don't need anything from them."

Surprisingly, they were nothing like me and my mother when it came to being materialistic. They were satisfied with the simplest of things.

Just when I wasn't looking for it, I finally found true love. Ironically, it was with someone I'd known for a really long time and as luck would have it, our paths crossed at just the right time. Mack was my cousin, Lenny's best friend and we hung out a lot during my summers down in New Orleans. He was going into his junior year at Gretna and seemed to be doing really well. He was clearly balling out of control and that was a complete turnoff for me at first because I was determined not to fall for another baller. But Mack was different. When he questioned me about my hesitancy to get involved with him, I was honest. I told him about Tyree and Little Ty and I even told him about the little trafficking operation. He said he suspected as much when he saw me rolling in my new whip. He promised to keep our relationship "business-free," telling me he would never allow me to get involved with anything like that. Whenever it was time for me to make one of my trips, I could tell he wasn't with it.

"Look Dana, we can put an end to this-- straight up. I don't want my woman going up and down the road like this; it's too dangerous."

But I was determined to maintain my independence.

"I'm good Mack, I promise."

Eventually, he stopped bringing it up. However he, he came up with another approach for dealing with the situation. I didn't know it at first, but Mack routinely had one of his boys to follow me during each of my trips. He did it to make sure that I was okay. It was a true gangster move and it pretty much sealed it for me when I found out. On one of my trips, things got sort of wiry when my connection started questioning me about the quantity of my delivery. I tried telling him that I was only a carrier and that I had no idea what was actually in the packages. I was delayed for over four hours, while I waited for the guy to straighten the mess out with Tyree. When I finally made it back to campus, Mack told me that he already knew why I was so late getting back to school. As it

Behind Closed Doors: *Dana's Story*

turned out, he had an entire crew enroute to the drop-off spot to join forces with the guy who was already there. I was given the go ahead to leave just minutes before they would have arrived.

"Do you know what would have happened if you hadn't left when you did? It wouldn't have been pretty, Dana. This shit has to stop. It's too dangerous," he said, hugging me so tightly, I could barely breathe. Mack was a true gangster in every sense of the word and he ran the campus like it belonged to him. The way he interacted with his peers and his confidence was like an aphrodisiac. The thing that really did it for me was his ability to turn it all off when it came to me. He allowed me to see the sensitive side of him, which was a perfect contrast to his other side.

Tyree was a little salty when he found out about Mack. Apparently, he had some spies on the yard or how else would he know? But I was ready for him when he confronted me.

"So you got yourself a little boyfriend, huh?"

"And you have a little girlfriend. I can't believe you're kicking it with that chicken head Ladasia. Not only is she the biggest trick in East Boogie, she's my worst enemy...."

"Whoa now. Let's not forget, I found your ass on the stripper pole."

"You might have found me on the stripper pole, but Ladasia couldn't fit on a stripper pole if she tried. Don't even use her name in the same sentence with mine," I said, going for blood.

Of all people in the world, this was the one he chose. I was actually more offended than anything else. At the moment, I couldn't care less about the fact that he was kicking it with someone else, but he could have at least chosen someone with a little more class.

Ladasia was the one chick that Ja'El and I had to check on a regular basis. The rest of the girls got the message during our junior high school days, when Ja'El and I became known for our fighting skills. For some reason, Ladasia was determined to prove everyone wrong. For a fleeting moment, I wanted to get my hands on her and give her a good ass whipping just for old time's sake.

"Knock it off Dana. Ladasia doesn't mean anything to me and you know that."

"Whatever Tyree--she was my worst enemy and you knew it," I said quietly.

When he failed to say anything, I continued.

"But if that's how you wanna roll, it's all good. Yes, I have a boyfriend. From now on, our relationship is business only."

Under normal circumstances, I'm sure my comment would have resulted in some serious consequences--like the loss of a vehicle. However, I wasn't worried about that. His reason for giving me the car was business-related in the first place. I was his number one runner and the car was vital to the entire operation. He finally chilled and respected my wishes. From then on, it was strictly business.

****

Alex

It was hard to believe that Dana and I were the same age. She sort of reminded me of the chick from Cleopatra Jones because of the way the way she carried herself. But underneath the hardcore exterior, I sensed there were multiple layers of pain. She talked about her friend Ja'El and Little Ty a lot and I could tell she really loved her father and the rest of her family, but she never mentioned her mother. I was never one to pry, but I was a very talented listener. Whenever Dana got in the mood to share, I just listened.

Once we got our class schedules down, we incorporated the party aspect of college life. I called it multi-tasking. By the end of spring semester, Dana was booed up with a dude named Mack who happened to be a friend of her cousin Lenny from New Orleans. Mack was an upperclassman and he was extremely rough around the edges. Rumor had it that he was at the center of all of the illegal activities around campus. I totally believed the rumor because he seemed a little too "well-established" for a college kid. The Volvo, the flashy clothes and the off-campus apartment, which was absolutely laid, were dead giveaways. Dana said his folks were well-off, but I had a feeling there was a little more to the story than that. In spite of his flaws, he absolutely adored Dana, and I figured that was all that really mattered.

"So Dana, what's up with your boyfriend back home? Did you break up with him or what?"

"I guess you could say that, Alex. I found out he was kicking it with my worst enemy from high school. As far as I'm concerned, it's over."

Although Dana was adamant about the fact that things were over with her and Tyree, she still maintained contact with him. She even skipped a few Friday classes to make the trip back to East St Louis and I assumed her purpose was to see him. When she returned from those trips on Sunday, she would sleep for hours and on Monday mornings, we'd take a trip over to the bank. None of this ever registered as anything out of the ordinary to me--that is until Dana got one of those informative phone calls from home in the spring our sophomore year. I could tell this particular call was unlike any of the other ones.

"Look, Mellow, I hope you didn't call to tell me anything else about Ladasia and Tyree 'cause I don't give a damn," she said.

"No, Dana, this is some serious shit. I need you to listen and listen good," Mellow said on the other end of the phone.

"Okay, I'm listening. What's up?"

"When was the last time you made a drop for your boy?"

"'Bout a month ago, why?"

"That's what I thought. Ain't nothing moving through East Boogie right now. I heard something about a secret indictment that's about to go down any day. If what I'm hearing is true, the feds may be headed your way."

"The feds? What the hell do they have to do with it?"

"Interstate trafficking Dee--you had to cross at least three state lines. That's fed time."

"So basically, you're telling me I'm going to jail."

"Yes, and from the looks of it, your boy set you up to take the fall. One more thing Dana, I think I know who killed Ja'El."

Dana took a deep breath and sat down on the edge of her bed. Tyree obviously failed to mention the minor detail about federal drug-trafficking laws when he brought her into this mess. Interstate trafficking was a serious offense.

Behind Closed Doors: *Dana's Story*

When she got off the phone, she filled in the gaps. She told me about the abuse from her mom and Mr. James, her other son, becoming a drug mule, her father's incarceration and she elaborated on her mother's addiction to heroin. And I thought I had issues. I kind of understood the long-term effects of abuse from personal experience, but my story was nothing compared to Dana's. When she asked me to look out for her family, I had to say yes.

Dana's friend was right. She was arrested three days later.

Chapter Twelve
True To The Game

I couldn't get mad at anyone except myself. I was very much aware of the risks and I chose to roll the dice.

I was arrested and placed in handcuffs while standing in the lobby of my dorm. I could hear the whispers from my fellow dormmates, "I knew she was doing something illegal," one girl said.

I vaguely recall Alex's response, but when she was finished reading that chick, no one said another word.

"It's all good Alex," I said, trying to calm my friend. She was more upset than I was about the chatter in the hallway.

"Hold it down for me. I'll be in touch soon."

From there, the feds executed their warrant to search my "living space." Thankfully, Alex anticipated this. The night before my arrest, she insisted that I pack up all of my valuable gear and cart it down to the basement of the dorm, which served as a storage area for residents. At some point, she would put everything into an off campus storage facility.

"If anything happens to me or we lose contact before you get out, that's where it will be," Alex said. She might have been a little green, but she was smart as hell and destined to be one hell of an attorney.

The thing that worried me the most about the situation was the impact it would have on my family. They would be okay financially; thanks to Alex, but there were so many other issues to consider. I gave Alex the account information and blank checks for the account that I opened in my sister's name. There was enough money in the account to take care of my family for at least two years. I talked to Lenny the day before my arrest and told him what was going down. He'd already gotten the news from Mack, who was beside himself with anger at Tyree. Lenny promised to look out for Granny and the kids as well. The thing that bothered me the most was the fact that I was placing additional burden and heartache on my grandmother. To see me locked up and to know that my mother was probably on her last leg as a result of her heroin addiction could have resulted in my grandmother's un-doing, but not this lady.

"I was afraid something like this would happen. I knew that boy was no good the moment I laid eyes on him. Just do your time Dana and don't worry about us. We'll be right here when you get out," she said.

She respected my wishes for her not to attend any of the court proceedings. I didn't want her to see me shackled and handcuffed. I figured it was pointless anyway, since I was choosing not to fight the charges. The public defender was sure I'd lost my mind when I informed him of my plan.

"Miss Toussaint, you're looking at a maximum of 20 years for a conspiracy charge."

It was my first time hearing the actual charges, and they sounded pretty serious, but my mind was mad up.

"I appreciate your concern, Attorney Gallagher, but...."

"Okay, let me break it down for you Dana--I can call you Dana, right?" he asked, quickly cutting me off before I could defend my decision and quickly proceeding before I could respond to his question.

"The feds aren't after you Dana; I think you're smart enough to know that. They want Tyree. Keep in mind, they didn't catch you physically transporting anything. Right now, all you have is a conspiracy charge, so you have a good chance to beat this thing or at least get a lighter sentence."

"I'm aware of that, sir."

"I need you to understand something else Dana. Federal drug trafficking is a crime of weights and measurements. They're telling me they have evidence to prove that you moved no less than five kilos across three state lines on several different occasions. That kind of weight could get you some serious time. Give them something, Dana--anything, and I can get you home within six months," my handsome Jewish attorney pleaded.

"If not, you're looking at ten to life."

"First of all, I'm not a snitch. It's just not in my DNA. I did the crime and I'm willing to do the time. Second of all, what kind of life do you think I would have if I rolled on Tyree? I got into this mess to take care of my family, so I'm not about to put their lives in danger to get out of it," I said thinking about what happened to Ja'El's family.

"This is the hand I was dealt, so they're my cards to play. I gotta play 'em the way I see fit." I found myself making that statement far more than I cared to admit.

"Based on your statement, I assume you're aware of the fact that Tyree set you up to take this fall."

"I'm aware of that, sir. But karma is a bitch. He'll get it back with interest."

In a last ditch effort to change my mind, Attorney Gallagher gave me a quick historical lesson on mandatory minimums, going all the way back to 1986. I was in junior high school, but I vaguely recalled the story about Len Bias, the college basketball star. The sudden death of the star athlete from an apparent cocaine overdose was the catalyst for increased political involvement in the 'war on drugs'. Congressional implementation of mandatory minimum sentencing for drug trafficking was the end result.

"Dana, these laws were supposedly written to fix this country's drug problem. I don't need to tell you the plan failed. Had it worked, you wouldn't be here. You wanna know what really happened?"

"Sure," I said, genuinely interested in the rest of his lesson, but sure that nothing he had to say would change my mind.

"It was a political move, Dana, implemented during an election year. The politicians couldn't have cared less about Len Bias or any other Black kid losing their life to drugs. The Democrats controlled congress at the time and they were looking for ways to maintain control. Taking credit for a major anti-drug program was an excellent way to do it. The speaker of the house at the time was Tip O'Neal. He happened to be a native of Boston and as luck would have it, Len Bias was headed to the Celtics. The country was outraged over Bias' death and O'Neal capitalized on it. The mandatory sentences were implemented to target high-level drug offenders. However, the bulk of the impact is dispersed among low level offenders like yourself. For example, 5 grams of cocaine is equivalent to about 25 rocks and a few hundred dollars on the street, yet it'll get you a minimum of 5 years in jail. On the other hand, it takes 500 grams of powder cocaine to get the same sentence. Are you with me?", he asked.

I nodded my head and he continued.

Behind Closed Doors: *Dana's Story*

"Dana, these laws are designed to keep people like you behind bars. I don't want to see you become a statistic."

My attorney seemed to be very genuine in his efforts to help me. Judging from the expensive suit and fancy shoes, I figured he was probably a rich do-gooder, whose sole purpose in life was to help individuals such as myself. It had to be the case, because public defenders clearly couldn't afford to wear Armani suits.

"I appreciate you for taking the time to explain all of this to me, but I don't have a choice".

When I refused to roll on Tyree, the federal drug trafficking charge was officially added to the conspiracy charge. As a first time offender charged with transporting more than five kilos, I was looking at ten years to life plus twenty years on the conspiracy charge. Thankfully, my attorney was able to pull a few strings and managed to get the weight reduced to 4.9 kilos. Technically it was still 5 kilos; but apparently, the judge decided to give me a break. The sentencing guidelines for anything less than five kilos, was five to forty years. I got 6 years in the federal pen.

In spite of the many spoils of the drug game, women are rarely the ultimate beneficiaries. This was painfully obvious when I became acquainted with the other ladies in my cellblock. Like me, a majority of the inmates were also doing time for their involvement in their boyfriends' or husbands' drug operations. The introduction of mandatory sentencing to the federal drug laws in the mid-1980s had already resulted in an increase in the number of Black women in the prison system by 800%. In addition, women routinely incurred longer sentences due to their refusal or inability to provide valuable evidence about their significant other's involvement in the crime.

One chick, named Claudine, was doing five years for improper use of the telephone. Apparently, she answered a few phone calls at her home that were linked to actual drug deals. When she couldn't provide any valuable information against her boyfriend, she was forced to take the fall for the entire operation. Her boyfriend got probation. Something was seriously wrong with that picture. The flaws within the criminal justice system allowed this sort of thing to happen on a regular basis.

Behind Closed Doors: *Dana's Story*

I began serving my sentence on June 10, 1993. The first few days were like an out of body experience for me. My brain was somehow disconnected from my body as I instinctively followed the commands of those in charge. I felt like a robot. Three other ladies in-processed with me. After disrobing completely, we were issued new bras, panties, socks and gray canvas deck shoes. The gray shoes were an indication of status according to time served. Red shoes were reserved for inmates with five or more years behind bars. After changing into the facility-issued khaki pants and shirts, we were lined up for fingerprinting and received our federal prison identification number. Next, we were taken to the medical unit and given a head to toe exam. Once our physicals were complete, we were taken to the commissary and issued bed linen, two sets of pajamas and three additional sets of khakis. I was told in advance to bring at least $300 for the commissary because I would need it to purchase my personal hygiene items, extra towels, sweat suits and tennis shoes. The money was gone in no time, so I asked Mack to place an additional three hundred dollars on my books. My plan was to make do with about fifty dollars a month or six hundred per year.

From there, we attended the new inmate orientation class, where we were given a lecture on the rules and regulations of the facility: keep off the grass, identification on your person at all times, beds made by 7 am, breakfast by 7:20 and showers in the evenings. After the lecture, we were taken on a tour of the facility, which included the common room, the cafeteria, and the library.

There were four women to each cell. Since there were only four of us being in-processed that day, we were all assigned to the same room. So much for privacy, I thought, eyeing the incredibly small living space and thinking about the very first letter I received from my father.

"Privacy doesn't exist when you're locked up Dana—it's in your head. Keep your mind occupied," was the opening line in the letter. He closed the letter with a quote from Malcolm X.

"...In all our deeds, the proper value and respect for time determines success or failure."

Those two statements alone would get me through the next six years.

Behind Closed Doors: *Dana's Story*

The only bright side to my ordeal was the fact that I was in better contact with my father than I'd ever been. I received a letter from him at least once a week and I always responded to it the same day. He was an incredibly intelligent man, full of wisdom for the way things should have been. How in the world did he end up with someone like my mother? She was just plain shallow. Intelligent conversation was one of the things that my parent's relationship lacked.

Within the first few weeks of my incarceration, I was fully immersed in my new environment. I knew which ladies were cool and which ones to avoid; the same was true for the prison guards. I figured conflict with a bunch of hardened criminals or a run in with one of the guards was the last thing I needed because my goal was to do my time and not a day over. Ja'El and Alex were the only real friends I ever had and I was accustomed to rolling no more than one deep at any given time. As a result, I didn't have a problem keeping to myself. However, I quickly realized I had to find something constructive to keep me occupied or I would end up in the psych unit. After getting over the initial shock of being locked up, I enrolled in a couple of college courses in order to make good on my promise to my father and Alex about getting my degree. When I wasn't doing classwork, I was writing in my journal. I decided to chronicle my daily experiences along with a few lines dedicated to my son. I figured when the time came for me to explain my absence, I would have tangible evidence to offer my son as proof that I didn't leave him intentionally.

Tyree and my mother were both missing in action throughout my entire ordeal. Tyree hadn't even bothered to thank me for not ratting him out to the feds, but I wasn't surprised. As far as I was concerned, they no longer existed.

Behind Closed Doors: *Dana's Story*

Chapter Thirteen
Amina Dyamond

I met Ongell Lorenz Jackson aka Amina Dyamond on "zero day", which was our first day of incarceration in the federal penitentiary. I called it "zero day" because the clock didn't start ticking until midnight. With four people cramped in such a small space, it was impossible not to interact to some degree. The other two girls bonded extremely fast, which left Amina and me to ourselves. As a loner, I wasn't keen on forming quick relationships with complete strangers. I suppose the sentiment was a remnant of my experiences in East Boogie--the smaller the circle the better. Amina obviously felt the same way. Her head was always buried in a spiral notebook. Sometimes her writing would become so fierce that she'd end up breaking the lead of her pencil each time she wrote a word. Curiosity finally got the best of me one day while sharing a table in the library. What the hell was she writing about?

"If you don't mind me asking, what are you writing?" I asked.

"Lyrics."

"What kind of lyrics?" I asked, thinking what a dumb question.

"Rap lyrics, but I prefer calling it poetry."

"Wow, so that's what's up? You're an aspiring rap artist."

"Yep that's what's up. I got six years in this joint. When I get out, I'm gonna have lyrics for days."

"So how did you end up in here?"

"I needed money for studio time, so I got involved with some cats who said they could help me make some quick money. Come to find out, these guys were in over their heads and didn't even know it. They were just some low-level dealers for one of the drug operations in South Memphis. They asked me to run a few keys for 'em, which was cool the first few times and I got five grand for each trip."

Five grand. I thought about the ten grand I was getting each time I crossed the Texas state line. Tyree's generosity in the midst of his evil ways never ceased to amaze me. As a matter of fact, it was just downright confusing.

"The feds got me on my fourth trip," Amina continued. "I got caught carrying three keys. When they started questioning me, I realized I didn't even have real names for the guys who gave me the dope to carry. Of course they didn't believe me. Who in their right mind would be stupid enough to do such a thing? To this day, they still think I'm withholding evidence; when in reality, I don't know jack-shit."

"Wow. Seems like we're all doing time on jacked-up drug charges."

"What's your story?"

"Similar to yours except I was dating the dude that got me into this. On top of that, we have a kid together and he's married. I didn't find that out until after I had my son. He's at home chilling with his wife and kids and I'm doing time for him. They think I'm withholding evidence too, which is partially true. I refused to roll on my baby's father, but to be honest, I knew nothing about the actual operation.

"It's really the perfect crime. Keeping us in the dark is ingenious. Not only does it render us defenseless, it gives them the freedom to take risks they wouldn't ordinarily take."

Amina nailed it. Why else would Tyree have me carrying so much weight when he knew it could result in a life sentence if I got caught? From his perspective, the benefits clearly outweighed the risk.

Amina and I became fast friends after that conversation. It was apparent to me that music was really her passion and she was determined to get into the rap game if it was the last thing she did. I mentioned Tyree's transient brush with fame, and how his artist Mr. Robert kicked him to the curve and blew up within six months. He was devastated because of all the money he'd invested in studio time and radio promotions. His former artist was currently on the radio every time he turned it on.

"Dayum!!!!I know your boy must be mad as hell. Mr. Robert is the hottest thing on the radio right now."

"Yeah, he finally stopped listening to the radio altogether."

"Is he still in the music business?"

"Who knows? I haven't heard from him since my arrest."

"You know how to get in touch with him?"

Behind Closed Doors: *Dana's Story*

"Yeah, but I don't have shit to say to him."

"Word. Just remember, keep your friends close and your enemies closer. You never know."

Amina was a very complex individual. She attended college for a few semesters and her major was philosophy. She was always trying to find a deeper meaning for everything, which was a little annoying at times. However, I had to admit, most of what she said made a lot of sense. Before her incarceration, she called herself "Dyamond." She changed her name to Amina Dyamond after a few days of being locked up.

"Okay Amina. What's the deal with the name?"

I asked when she made a request for me to start calling her Amina Dyamond.

"Amina is an Arabic name that is frequently used in African culture. I chose the name because of its meaning: loyal, truthful, and trustworthy. The African Queen, Amina, was a fierce Muslim warrior as the legend goes, and she was "as capable as a man." As a very small child, Queen Amina's grandmother once caught her holding a dagger and "emulating a warrior," she explained.

When I listened to some of Amina Dyamond's stories about her childhood, I was convinced she'd chosen the right name. She stood about 5'3 and weighed a little over 120 pounds, but according to her, she was known as the knockout queen in her hood.

"I had to bust a few heads Dana but after that, it was all good with the females on my block."

In spite of the reputation she earned as a fighter, Amina's biggest claim to fame on the street was her ability to freestyle or recite lyrics that were not previously composed. In the mid-80's to early 90's, the ability to freestyle was one of the things that set rappers apart--either you had it or you didn't. Amina was born and raised in the South Bronx, which according to her, is the holy mecca for hip-hop. Our cellblock was heavily populated with chicks from Brooklyn and Queens and they adamantly disagreed with her every time the subject came up, each claiming their own hood as the birthplace of hip-hop. Amina's love for hip-hop began in middle school while hanging out with her older sister Angel. By junior-high, she was reciting her own rhymes and battling other females whenever the opportunity presented itself. At some point, the

Behind Closed Doors: *Dana's Story*

female rappers finally gave in to the fact that she was the princess of freestyle and eventually the dudes started backing down as well. After junior high, Amina's family moved to Memphis, where hip-hop was still in its infancy. For Amina, the move was like taking milk from a baby or removing oxygen from the earth--it was incompatible with life. Although she was basically torn away from the environment that defined her very existence, her love for hip-hop always remained.

    I was no expert when it came to identifying musical talent, but I could appreciate the poetic artistry in Amina's lyrics. She was what I would call a conscientious rapper because she had a knack for telling Afrocentric tales and metaphorically describing the social injustices within our culture. After reading pages and pages of Amina's work, I was convinced that the mainstream media and snooty English professors were way off the mark with their negative views concerning rap music. Rap lyrics and poetry were one and the same. They shared the same literary devices; such as assonance and alliteration, where the use of vowel and consonant repetition are the foundations of creativity. So why then, is rap not considered a true literary art form? Perhaps it's because of the increased value of written language over spoken language in Western Cultures. That was one of the popular mainstream excuses. Like most of the arguments against rap music as a true artistic form, this one was crazy as well. I suppose it was plausible, but I wasn't buying it.

    Other critics argue that rap lyrics are primarily incomplete without a beat or incapable of standing alone. According to this group of critics, a poet's ability to create passionate and sensitive expressions through words that resonate without music was the difference between the two. Complete bullshit. Amina's lyrics were dope with or without music.

    Finding success in the music industry was not an easy task for female rappers. In all honesty, I could see how Amina's passion for hip-hop would have played a role in her current situation. At the time of her arrest, she was just two songs short of completing her demo and needed the money for studio time. She was busted during what she said would have been her last drop. Talk about bad luck. In spite of it all, Amina was still determined to make it in the rap game--"by any means necessary". Until then, she planned to spend every waking moment honing her craft.

Amina and I were tight for the rest of our incarceration. She had my back and I had hers. A huge portion of our time was used to plot and plan our revenge, but most importantly, we wanted to correct our wrongs. The rest of the time was spent refining Amina Dyamond's sound. I was able to get my hands on a hand-held CD player; thanks to Mack, which allowed Amina to stay abreast of the current hip-hop trends. Her lyrics over the fresh new industry sound were straight dope.

Chapter Fourteen
Karma--The List

Six years was equivalent to 72 months, 313 weeks, 2,190 days, 52,560 hours, 3.1 million minutes and 189 million seconds. That was the amount of time that I had to figure out how to even the score with the individuals who ruined my life. I wouldn't consider myself to be a vengeful person and I rarely held a grudge; but whenever I allowed myself to replay all of the horrible events that occurred in my life, revenge was the only thing that made sense. At the top of the list was my mother--the ringleader. She was the catalyst for all of it. I guess the old saying that blood is thicker than water was true because try as I might, I couldn't bring myself to think of harming her in any way. However, I had a feeling she would reap what she'd sown. What goes around always comes back around. Next on my list was Mr. James followed by Tyree and the animals who took Ja'El's life.

Mid-way into my sentence, we got another inmate from East Boogie. It was Ladasia. Mellow had already informed me of her pending arrival and I had compiled a long list of ways to make her life a living hell. But when she finally showed up, I took one look at her and lost my desire to do her any harm. I immediately recalled dissing her to Tyree when I found out they were kicking it and I distinctly remember calling her fat. Back then, she was literally two biscuits away from morbid obesity. Her appearance that day was the exact opposite--she was probably 105 pounds soaking wet. Mellow failed to mention that Ladasia went from being Tyree's ride or die to being East Boogie's latest rock star. She was so strung out that she didn't even recognize me when I approached her in the cafeteria.

"Ladasia Perkins," I said, as I stood behind her in the salad line. "Remember me?"

"Why should I remember you?"

She took a quick look and I was convinced she didn't have a clue.

"It's, Dana."

After a few seconds, she slowly turned around and gave me a classic "deer in the headlights" look.

"Dana Toussaint," she whispered.

"Yes, Dana Toussaint."

I answered in spite of the fact that her comment was a statement and not a question. A part of me wanted to grab her by the neck and squeeze the life out of her, but the compassionate side of me prevented me from doing so. She was clearly as much a victim as I was.

"How much time do you have?"

"Twenty to life," she said.

She looked around and tried her best to stop the tears from making it to the surface of her eyes.

"Twenty to life? Wow," I breathed.

I sympathized with her even more after that sobering piece of information and wondered if I could have done that much time. In my opinion, Ladasia didn't have a snowball's chance in hell to make it out of there in one piece. She was mentally, and in her current state, physically incapable of doing it. First of all, she was an addict and this place was stocked with every type of drug you could think of. My guess was she'd get caught up in the wrong crowd and become an incarcerated, drugged-out zombie.

"What happened, Ladasia? Last I heard, you and Tyree were balling out of control and setting people up."

I wanted to let her know that I was aware of her role in my demise.

"You know exactly what happened, Dana--Tyree happened. He lured me in by telling me that I was prettier than you and that I deserved to have all of the things that you had. When he told me I was in a position to take your place altogether, I was in, no questions asked. Funny thing was, he couldn't stop talking about you. I swear, if I didn't know any better, I would have thought he had real feelings for you. You were like his blueprint. Me and all of the other females were in competition with you and you weren't even around.

"So, how did you end up using?"

I took the subject off of my relationship with Tyree even though I wanted to further explore her comment. However, I wasn't prepared to hear anything she had to say about my relationship with Tyree. No sense trying to understand something that no longer mattered to me. Besides, I was curious about Ladasia's descent into addiction. Believe it or not, Tyree hated drugs. After I quit using coke, I wanted to try marijuana because it seemed to keep Miss Cookie in a really good place. He wasn't having it.

"I'd already tried coke when we hooked up and it sort of went from there," she said. "On top of that, he was constantly making comments about my weight. That's how I ended up smoking rocks--I wanted to be skinny. I thought I could control the drug, but as you can see, I was wrong."

"And Tyree never tried to stop you?"

"No," she said softly. "I found myself doing all sorts of stuff to outshine you, but none of it ever worked. Eventually, I went from doing the money exchange to doing drug runs after you got busted. I volunteered for it."

"Really?"

I silently thanked God that Tyree cared enough to stop me from going down that particular road.

"In hindsight, I realize he never gave a damn about me, Dana. I guess this is my punishment for stepping to him in the first place. I knew he was kicking it with you, but I was so jealous of you back in school. It just seemed like you had everything, even before Tyree came along. I hated you, so I purposely set out to steal your man."

None of this came as a surprise. However, she'd used the term "jealousy" inappropriately. Jealousy occurs when something you already have is threatened by a third person. Envy was a better choice of words because it refers to wanting something someone else has. Like she said, her ill feelings toward me were in place long before Tyree entered the pictured. She envied my appearance, my material possessions, and eventually, my man. If only she'd known what I had to do to get those new Jordan's back in high school.

After hearing Ladasia's account of the way things went down, I was convinced that Tyree would have made an excellent pimp. He obviously had a smooth tongue. This was perhaps the most essential attribute of a pimp. I could think of no less than twenty Iceberg quotes that would apply to Tyree, but the one that summed it up the best went something like this,

Behind Closed Doors: *Dana's Story*

"...the most successful men I know with women are cold blooded with women."

Tyree was definitely cold-blooded.

I tried to help Ladasia as much as I could, but it was useless. She was a walking time bomb. As I predicted, she didn't have the mental fortitude to survive a twenty-year bid. The top three methods of prison suicide were strangulation, drug overdose, and self-inflicted wounds. I'd seen all of them. I think the one that bothered me the most was the chick who got her hands on a glass bottle, which she managed to break into tiny little pieces. As the story goes, she spent an entire day swallowing the broken glass, which eventually perforated her bowel. I happened to be one of the individuals that walked into the bathroom when the "shit hit the fan"--literally. There was blood everywhere and at first, we thought she's been stabbed, but no external puncture wounds were found. The real story came a few days later from an inmate assigned to the infirmary. According to her, it took about 48 hours for the chick to finally bleed to death from a ruptured colon and sepsis. Surgeons were able to stop the bleeding, but the infection in her body was too widespread. Her death was quite painful. Ladasia took an easier route, but her method required a lot of planning and patience. She recalled reading about the Nazi's use of cyanide in the gas chambers during the Holocaust. Cyanide is a poison that quickly causes death by asphyxiation, if an adequate amount is ingested. After doing a little research, Ladasia discovered that apple seeds are a viable source of cyanide. Apparently, it takes about 143 apples to extract a half a cup of crushed apple seeds, which is a lethal dose of cyanide. Drinking the seeds too slowly or not drinking enough seeds could result in a sub-lethal dose or possible brain damage and the person could end up in a vegetative state for the rest of their life. Witnesses said that Ladasia gulped down an entire cup of crushed apple seeds in a few seconds flat. She chose the method because it was supposedly quick and painless. She was right.

Before she took her own life, Ladasia answered one of the questions that continued to haunt me. Why did Tyree turn on me?

"Just to let you know, Dana, Tyree was not the one that called the shots when you got busted. It was his wife. She found out about you and your son and she gave Tyree an ultimatum. She wanted you dead, but jail was a good enough alternative for her."

"How did she find out?"

"Tyree and his wife are an extremely odd couple. She's an officer in the military and he's a drug dealer. According to him, they were high-school sweethearts. Anyway, she was hip to his involvement in the drug game; but when she noticed a sudden change in his behavior, she began investigating. When she found out about you and your son, she threatened to take the kids and make sure he never saw them again. He had no choice."

Her description of the way things went down made a lot of sense. Perhaps the explanation should have made me feel a little better or less confused, but it didn't. He chose his wife and their kids over Little Ty and me. That was the bottom line.

I was three years into my sentence and close to completing my degree in criminal justice of all things. With a felony drug conviction, my chances to find work in the field would be slim to none, but Alex told me not to waste my time worrying about employment opportunities. If things went according to plan, she would be finished with law school by the time I was released and I could work for her. It was a cool offer and it gave me peace of mind knowing that I had something to fall back on.

My father was up for parole in eighteen months. He apologized a million times for bringing Tyree into my life.

"I should have known better than to trust a snake Dana," he wrote.

I constantly reminded him of the fact that everything in life happened for a reason. Tyree turned out to be a thorn in my side, but I could never forget the fact that he rescued me from a situation that could have been far more detrimental than a six-year prison sentence.

My mother was pretty much a lost cause. Mellow was keeping me up to date on the happenings in East Boogie, and according to him, nothing had changed with her. She was still in and out of rehab and fronting at the new methadone clinic that opened in East Boogie. Heroin is a hell of a drug. Even the strongest desire to get clean is no match for the persistent cravings of the drug, which can persist for years even after kicking the addiction.

The way things looked, I didn't think she would ever get clean. At some point, my hopes for seeing her clean gave way to acceptance and I prepared myself for the worse. The kids were my only concern. They were all doing well and thrived thanks to my grandmother. Dahlia graduated from high school and planned to pursue a career in social work. I was sure that our family dynamics had a lot to do with her decision. Little Ty was three years old and still too young to understand why I wasn't around. At some point, I knew the phone calls would not be enough. As much as I wanted to hold him in my arms, I couldn't allow him to see me locked up like an animal--which is the same thing my father did to me, my brother and my sisters. I guess the apple really doesn't fall far from the tree.

To be honest, I wasn't very keen on having any visitors other than Mack and Alex. But out of the blue, Mellow insisted on a visit. He had some pressing information that couldn't be shared over the phone.

"Dana, you know I don't do jailhouse visits for nobody," Mellow said.

"I know. That's the part I'm worried about. Whatever you have to say must be extremely important."

I went through the tedious process to place him on the visiting list and began the arduous task of trying to figure out what he had to say. I knew it wasn't about my mother because that was something he could discuss over the phone and he was well aware of the fact that news about Tyree was the last thing I wanted to hear. He must have gotten some information about Ja'El's killers. The information he gave me before I was arrested turned out to be false. Mellow made the journey from East Boogie to Bryan, Texas just days after being approved for visitation.

"Yo, Dee, you're looking good. What are they feeding you in here?"

Mellow grinned and checked out my new and improved physique, compliments of the prison gym. I was hitting the gym pretty hard, because aside from writing, it was the only thing that gave me any real satisfaction.

"Well, thanks, Mel. You should have caught me a couple weeks ago. I think I lost a few pounds worrying about your visit. What the hell is up?"

"Alright, here's the deal; I know who killed your girl...," he said.

He paused while he struggled to deliver the horrible news. After he gave me the three names, he went on to tell me that Ja'El had been raped. This was news to me. Ja'El's grandmother hadn't shared that piece of information when I visited her before the funeral. Apparently, the information was being withheld for investigative purposes. I was in complete shock over the rape, but the fact that I knew all three of the suspected murderers was an even harder pill to swallow.

"That's not all, Dana."

"I'm listening," I said, gritting my teeth and fighting to hold back the tears.

"Dana, they're saying your mom set the whole thing up."

I felt like someone had just kicked me in the stomach. According to Mellow's second-hand account, my mother was in pretty bad shape after Tyree put an end to her arrangement with Mr. James. For a junkie like her, to lose a steady supply of dope and her source of income was a death sentence. She knew about the gig that Ja'El and I had at the strip club and she knew that Ja'El stashed her money for college. She approached three of her junkie friends to hit Ja'El's house for the loot. The hit was supposed to take place when Ja'El's uncles were away from home and no one was supposed to get hurt. The three geniuses showed up at the house at the worst possible moment and things went downhill from there. The rest was history.

"Mellow, you're telling me my mother is responsible for all of this? Are you absolutely sure?"

"It's true, Dee. Your mom skipped town the next day and the three amigos disappeared for a while too."

"Who's your source? I need proof."

"It's true, Dana. I wouldn't be here if I wasn't sure."

Anger is an extremely overwhelming emotion and revenge is the primitive response to it. In the weeks and months that followed Mellow's visit, I tried everything from reading my Bible to participating in the anger management sessions that were held three times a week. The Bible proved to be too confusing--one section says "an eye for an eye" and a few chapters over it says, "repay no one evil for evil." The anger management class didn't help much either. I got tired of hearing, "you can't change what happened," so I quit going to the classes. Vengeance is an extremely complex emotion and one that is best served cold. In other words, I had three years remaining on my sentence to simmer over everything that happened. The time gave me an opportunity to come up with a rational plan to address all of the individuals who played a role in ruining my life; and above all, it prevented me from acting on my emotions.

Mack was a consistent source of strength for me. When I told him about Ja'El's killers, he promised to "take care of it." I believed him. His words allowed me to sleep at night.

Epilogue

June 4, 1999. We had less than a week left on our six-year sentences. Once released, we were required to complete an additional thirty days in a halfway house at an approved location. We were both granted permission for re-location to New Orleans. After six years of trying to figure out what to do with the rest of our lives, it was finally time to execute our plan.

Amina was still very passionate about her dreams to become a hip-hop artist and I was going to be her manager. Tyree still dabbled in the music industry and was determined to find the world's greatest entertainer. Amina definitely fit the bill. I figured since he owed me a favor for not selling him out on the drug charge, it was time to cash in. But first, we had to complete her demo tape. Once Tyree got a taste of Amina, he would be sold. Getting Amina into the rap game was only a small piece to the puzzle. I had big plans for Tyree due in part to some information that I got from Ladasia. In the days that lead up to her death, she must have felt the need to purge. Before everything was said and done, Tyree would regret the day he decided to cross me and he wouldn't be the only one.

The day finally came. I didn't sleep at all the night before, with so many thoughts floating in my head. I couldn't wait to see my family. Six years of telephone calls and pictures had been my only contact between with my family. How would Little Ty respond to me? Could he ever forgive me for my absence?

"Ongell Jackson and Dana Toussaint. Today's your lucky day," the prison guard smirked.

She held out the "get out of jail outfits" that we'd purchased a few months back.

"Looks like you got family coming down for your release. I hope they're aware of the fact that transportation from here to your final destination is provided by our facility."

"Yes, they're aware."

"Well what are you waiting for? You got thirty minutes to shower and get dressed," she said with a bigger smile.
She was one of my favorite guard because she seemed to really care about us.

I was ready in fifteen minutes and sat on the edge of my bunk. Amina was right behind me.

"I can't believe we're really leaving, Dana."

"Yeah, I know. I'm afraid I'll wake up and discover this is all a dream."

"Grab your things, ladies. It's time to go," the guard said.

Amina and I both had one laundry bag apiece, mostly filled with pictures and mail. We left our clothes, shoes and other personal items to anyone that wanted them. The gesture almost caused a huge brawl as the ladies scrambled to claim our "valuable" items.

Amina's family decided not to make the trip down to Texas, opting instead to await our arrival in New Orleans. I tried to persuade my family to do the same, but they weren't having it.

Alex was the first person that I saw when I turned the corner at the end of the long corridor. She hadn't changed a bit. She gave me a bear hug and stepped to the back of the line. Next in line was Mack, followed by Granny and my sisters. I couldn't believe how much they had grown; they were now beautiful young women. Next was my little brother, but I didn't see anyone else. Just when I was about to panic, my father stepped around the corner with Miss Cookie and two boys. Little Ty, who was almost eight years old, was the mirror image of his father. The other little boy was unfamiliar to me. I stood frozen as my father grabbed my hand and reached for the boys. In his thick Haitian accent, my father said the words that would change my life forever.

"Boys, this is your mother."

Redemption

Behind Closed Doors: *Dana's Story*

****

At first, I didn't know if I'd heard my father correctly.

I had hundreds of pictures of Little Ty, so I knew exactly who he was. However, I had no frame of reference for the other little boy. As I examined him closer, I realized he was the masculine version of me from his skin tone, hair color, the shape of his eyes--everything. When the tears began to flow, I grabbed both boys and held on for dear life.

"I'm so sorry."

Those were the only words that I could form. I had dreamt of that day and I had list of things that I planned to say if and when the opportunity ever presented itself. However, at that moment, I was speechless. When I realized the boys held on to me just as tight as I held them, time stood still and my heart began to overflow with joy. I made a silent vow that nothing would ever separate me from my children again.

"Dana, this is your son, Isaiah."

My father's voice was thick with tears.

"How did you find him?"

I found my voice and asked the question in between sobs.

"We will explain everything when we get home," he said with a smile.

As the guards approached to take us to the transport van, I sighed in regret because I didn't want to leave my family. From there, they would take us to the Greyhound station for the six-hour drive to New Orleans.

As we said our goodbyes, I hugged the boys tightly and explained the process to them again. I wanted them to know for certain that I was in their lives to stay.

I was an emotional wreck by the time we reached the bus station. To walk away from my kids was the hardest thing I ever had to do. They were so close, yet so far away. We had an hour-long wait before our departure, so we purchased our tickets and found two empty seats.

"Dana, I'm so happy for you."

Amina's hushed whisper broke the silence.

"Girl, I'm still in shock."

I shook my head in disbelief while my brain continued to replay the entire scene over and over again. How had they managed to find him after all this time? The past washed over me, and I couldn't stop the words that fell from my lips.

"My mother is evil, Amina. For the past thirteen years, I've conditioned myself to accept the fact that I would never see my son again. To be honest with you, I thought she put him in a dumpster. I can't believe he's alive."

Once again, the tears flowed freely and I allowed it.

When I finished the second round of tears, another bus pulled into the station. I was relieved to find it was the one bound for New Orleans. As we made our way towards the bus, I kept looking over my shoulder to see if there were any lurking prison officials waiting for us to make a wrong move. We probably looked like a couple of escaped cons because Amina looked over her shoulder as well.

Although we were no longer physically confined to the prison, we were mentally confined to the system. During the transitional briefing, the warden made it perfectly clear that even the slightest infraction would result in a violation of our release and possible re-incarceration. Once the bus started to move, I took a deep breath and relaxed.

The conditions of our release included a mandatory thirty-day stay in a halfway house, which was meant for transitional purposes only. Since Amina and I completed the entire term of our six-year sentences, the completion of the thirty-day stint meant we were officially done. An early release would have resulted in mandatory supervision or parole for an extended period of time. Neither of us found that option attractive. We had places to go and things to do, and nosey parole officers didn't fit into our plans.

We were instructed to check into the halfway house within the first thirty hours of release. Taking the six-hour bus ride into account, I had approximately twenty hours to spend with my family before I began the final stage of my nightmare. I opened the large brown envelope and read the instructions again.

Upon arrival to the facility, we would undergo drug and alcohol testing. For the first three days, we would be confined to the facility, and after that, we would begin our job search. The sooner we found employment, the better. Having a job would allow us to fly under the radar during our thirty day stay at the half-way house. That part would be easy enough. My Uncle Leonard had already hooked us up with a gig in his janitorial business. Instead of going to work, we would work on Amina's demo. I smiled at my reflection in the window as optimism began to replace the apprehension.

Chapter Fifteen
Home Sweet Home

Out of all of the things I'd been through during my six years of incarceration, the four hundred mile bus ride from Bryan, Texas to New Orleans proved to be the most traumatic. After being isolated from the world for such an extended period of time, the chaotic atmosphere of the Greyhound bus wreaked havoc on my nerves. The screaming babies, arguing couples, and irritable addicts in need of a long overdue hit of whatever poison they routinely placed in their veins, lungs, or stomachs was like an extension of our punishment. What difference would it make if we rode a bus or travelled with our families, as long as we reached our final destination at the appointed time? I figured it was either a control issue or a test. It would have been easy for us to ditch the bus in one of the little towns along the way. As tempting as it was, it probably would have resulted in a one-way ticket back to Bryan, Texas for violation of the transitional release protocols.

The illuminating skyline of the "Crescent City" created a brilliant mass of reflections from the Mississippi River, as we neared the city limits. My heart began to flutter. All of a sudden, the chaotic atmosphere of the Greyhound bus didn't matter anymore. I was almost "home."

We reached our final destination at around eight that night, and our families were at the bus station to await our arrival. After another round of hugs and some additional tears, we were on our way. Our first stop was Pat O'Brien's, one of my favorite restaurants and one of the oldest establishments in the French Quarter. The festive atmosphere was exactly what I needed, and while I'd never been much of a drinker, the restaurant's world renowned Hurricane was right on time. Our families laughed and got acquainted, but kept the conversation as light as possible. There would be plenty of time for heavy conversations later. We just wanted to enjoy the moment.

When the celebration was finally over, Amina and her family checked into a hotel near the halfway house while we made the much-anticipated journey to Granny's house. For years, her house had been a place of solace for me, and it was still the same. My sisters and I sat outside with Alex and Miss Cookie. We watched the boys compete in a few grueling rounds of Twenty-one under the lights with my Mack while my father refereed the game. It was the perfect opportunity for Alex to give me the details regarding my son Isaiah.

Apparently, my mother gave Isaiah to the "midwife" who delivered him. While I had frequent nightmares and vivid images of my mother placing my son in a dumpster, this had always been on my list of possibilities regarding what actually happened to my son. As it turns out, she gave him away because she didn't want the responsibility of caring for another child or a constant reminder of her evil deeds. The mid-wife was involved in a welfare scam and more kids meant more money from the system.

My mother named him Isaiah Toussaint and checked "unknown" in the paternity section of the form. Thankfully, she used my real name and listed me as the mother. That was how Alex managed to find him. After my mother completed the birth certificate information, she never looked back. The first ten years of Isaiah's life were pretty stable according to Alex. However, I'm sure there were some rough times. The midwife died suddenly when Isaiah was around nine, and the lady's daughter took him into her household. Without hesitation, she assumed responsibility for my son which included the welfare benefits. As Alex described the subsequent events, I imagined this lady was probably a prototypical welfare queen, like her mother. Most likely, her only ambition in life was to thoroughly work the system and force taxpayers to finance her existence. Her little hustle came to an end when one of her neighbors reported her to Child Protective Services for leaving the kids at home alone for extended periods of time. There were five kids in the home at the time ranging from ages four to nine years old, and Isaiah was the oldest. All of the kids were eventually placed in foster care and scattered across the city.

Alex contacted my father and my grandmother about a year before my scheduled release date to discuss the possibility of finding my son. She thought it would be a great homecoming surprise for me. She was absolutely correct, and her timing was perfect. She began her search around the same time Isaiah entered the foster care system, which coincided with the paper trail that would eventually lead her to my son. Mack and my father did a majority of the initial groundwork, gathering information about ghetto "midwives" and welfare hustlers dating back ten years. My sister Dahlia pitched in with some of the knowledge she'd gained from her college courses in Social Work. With the information they obtained, Alex was able to narrow the search to a specific group of potential suspects and began to contact Child Protective Services in those areas.

Alex was aware of all of my theories that concerned my son's fate, and after six months of dead-ends and wild goose chases, it seemed my greatest fear was a reality. She was glad that she'd opted not to say anything to me about the search. She decided that telling me about the search in advance would have set me up for yet another round of disappointment. She was right. To receive confirmation of my son's demise would have been the straw that broke the camel's back for me. Just when everyone was ready to throw in the towel, my grandmother made a suggestion.

"Someone has to go down there and find Diana. She has to know something," my grandmother said.

"That place is evil, Mrs. Ledoux. It destroyed my entire family," my father said.

He vowed he'd never set foot in East St Louis ever again, but under the circumstances, he felt obligated to reconsider. It was the least he could do.

"Where is she exactly? Do you know how to contact her?" he asked.

"I don't know exactly where she is, Bernard. I just know that she's still in East St Louis. If we're going to find Dana's son, we have to find Diana."

After a few phone calls, he and Mack were on a plane headed for East Boogie. Miss Cookie met them at the airport, and immediately drove them to my mother's last known location.

When they drove up to the place that my mother called home, everyone sat in silence and mentally prepared themselves for what would transpire. The "house" was really just a two-room shack with boarded up windows. It appeared to be nothing more than a detached garage that probably stood alongside an actual home at some point or another. However, the home was no longer there. After they checked out the surroundings for a few moments,

Mack realized he would have to take control of the situation. My father was visibly shaken by the prospect of what they had to face once on the other side of the door.

"You ready, Mr. Toussaint? "It's now or never." he asked.

My mother's nomadic lifestyle would make it difficult for them to find her again if she somehow slipped away.

"Let's go," my father said with a sigh.

The door wasn't locked, so after a few light taps with no response, Mack decided to enter. With the Beretta gripped in his right hand on the inside of his trousers, he slowly entered the room and called my mother's name.

"Diana."

There was no response, only slight movement from the three individuals who lay on makeshift beds in opposite corners of the room. My father gasped when he saw my mother. She was skin and bones. Her hair was matted, and her skin was three shades darker with the dirt and grime from years of neglect. She didn't see them at first, but when she heard my father's voice, she quickly sat up on the mattress.

"Diana..."

"Bernard, is that you?"

She narrowed and widened her eyes as if she' seen a ghost.

"Yes Diana, it's me," my father said shakily.

"Diana, won't you please let me get you some help?"

"Help? Is that what you came here for? Look at me Bernard. There ain't any help for me."

"Don't say that, Diana. As long as you're breathing, there's hope."

"Hope. Hope for what? My next fix? Right now, that's the only thing I'm hoping for. Just forget about me Bernard, and save your pity for somebody else," she said and began to lie back down.

"Diana, you can get clean again."

Miss Cookie jumped in, but she was quickly cut off. My mother turned toward her in a rage.

"Cookie, is that you? How dare you bring your trifling ass in here? I thought you were my friend, and you turned your back on me like everyone else. You like seeing me like this, don't you Cookie? You were always jealous of me. People tried to tell me, but I wouldn't listen. You couldn't wait for me to mess up so you could get your hands on Bernard. Bitch, I ain't dead yet, these streets don't keep no secrets. I know all about you and my husband. You violated the code, Cookie. I don't care how bad off I am right now, real friends NEVER cross that line. Now, get the hell out of here-- I mean it, Bernard. Get that bitch out of here now before I get up and whip her ass!"

"Diana, you got it all wrong..." my father tried to reason, but my mother wasn't interested.

It was one thing for him to see her like that, but to walk in there with the woman who stabbed her in the back? He was completely out of line.

"Both of you get the hell out of here," she interrupted before my father could finish.

"Let me talk to her alone," Mack whispered to my father.

Reluctantly, my father agreed. He searched my mother's eyes one last time and found nothing. He and Miss Cookie left the room, giving Mack an opportunity to work his magic.

"I'm a friend of Dana's, and we're trying to locate her son...her oldest son."

"How the hell am I supposed to know where the little bastard is?"

He was taken aback by my mother's careless attitude and instinctively, he wanted to grab her and shake some sense into her. How could she be so mean to her own flesh and blood? Thankfully, he realized it wasn't the right time or the right place to address the issue. The primary objective was to find Dana's son and Diana was the last resort. He finally understood what Dana tried to tell him for years. Although he'd listened, he never really grasped it completely. Her mother was pure evil. The humane approach wasn't a viable option, so he went with a tried and true method. It only took two twenty-dollar bills to find out everything he needed to know. He delivered the information to my father, but he kept that little part to himself. He felt guilty about giving her money because he knew what it would be used for, but then again, not giving her money wouldn't have prevented her from using. She was a junkie.

Mack contacted Alex with the information and Isaiah was located a few days later. He lived in what appeared to be a good foster home in Slidell, Louisiana. The family seemed to really care about the kids. It took another six months to complete all of the paper work and red tape required for my grandmother to obtain legal custody. That was a particularly delicate process and had to be handled with care in order to avoid any legal implications toward Diana. Alex handled all of the legal proceedings. In the end, the story given to the authorities implied that the child was born to a very young mother who willingly gave him to a family that would provide him with a good home. This couldn't have been furtherer from the truth, but the story served its purpose and Isaiah was finally placed into the care of my grandmother.

Chapter Sixteen
Searching for Answers

After talking to Alex, I got an overwhelming urge to speak with my grandmother. It was late, but I decided to go inside to see if she was still awake. When I entered the house, I found her sitting at the kitchen table listening to a gospel song that I recalled from my childhood. Since gospel music was the only music we were allowed to listen to during our summer visits, I had a list of songs I really liked. This particular song was one of my favorites. The name of the song was "Miracle" by the Jackson Southernaires, a traditional gospel quintet out of Jackson Mississippi. The song was actually a gut-wrenching story that was spoken over a solemn, melancholic gospel music arrangement. It was the story of a woman who was notified that her husband's plane had gone down in a crash and that there were no survivors. In spite of the horrible news, the woman and her children prayed for his safe return. At the end of the song, there's a knock at the door and the husband appears. No details were given in the song as to how he survived, but the message was clear--miracles still occur.

The song brought back so many memories. Some good, and some bad. That particular song gave me hope during some of my worst childhood experiences. The song convinced me that if I kept praying, my father would come to save me. Sometimes, I prayed so hard that my eyes would hurt. As the years passed, I finally conceded to the fact that my prayers were in vain because my father never came to my rescue. Eventually, I stopped praying altogether.

I imagined that my grandmother thought about my mother as she listened to this song. Most likely, she was still praying for a miracle. As it turned out, I was right.

"Dana, for the life of me I can't figure out where I went wrong with your mother. She was always a handful, but I never thought she would turn out like this."

She took a sip of tea and continued.

"When the doctor handed her to me, I broke down and started to cry. Everybody thought that they were tears of joy, but that wasn't the case entirely. Your mother was the spitting image of her father. She was the most beautiful baby I had ever seen in my life and I wasn't the only one who thought so. Her beauty mesmerized the entire nursing staff and they all fussed over who would get to hold her next. I finally had to put my food down and refused to let her out of my sight. I knew from experience that your mother had the type of beauty that was as much a blessing as it was a curse. I did what I could, Dana, but I guess it just wasn't enough."

"It's not your fault, Granny. It's not anyone's fault except her own. I've forgiven her because it was the only way for me to move on. The anger and bitterness almost killed me, so I had to let it go. I just wish I knew why, Granny. Why did she hate me so much?"

"I don't know, baby," she said.

Granny came over and hugged me. She pulled away and held me at arm's length.

"My greatest fear is never knowing why or at least getting a chance to ask her."

"Me too, Dana. That's the part that bothers me as well."

"Granny, do you think it was the drugs?"

"Baby, I've been around drug addicts all my life and ain't never heard tell of nothing like what your mother did to you. It had to be more than drugs."

We sat in silence for a few minutes lost in our own thoughts. My mind traveled back to a conversation that I had with Miss Angélique, the Haitian lady who seemed to be an expert on Black Magic. Could it be?

I decided to let it go for the moment. I had more pressing matters to discuss with my grandmother. I needed to let her know how much I appreciated all she'd done for me. Tears came to my eyes and I hugged her tighter.

"Granny, I don't know if I can ever thank you enough for everything you've done for me. Not once did you ever turn your back or give up on me. I promise, I'm going to make it up to you."

Uncontrollable sobs racked my body.

"There's no need to do anything Dana, except lead a happy and productive life with your kids. That's all I ask."

I just sat there with my head in her lap while she stroked my hair. I was really home.

"Which reminds me...," she said suddenly.

Startled at her quick movement, I sat up and faced her. She smiled and stroked my face gently.

"Come with me, Dana."

I followed her to the bedroom and took a seat on the huge king sized bed as she opened the door to her closet. After Granny dug around for a few minutes, she walked over to the bed and presented me with two shoe boxes. I opened the first box and found a bundle of cancelled checks neatly stacked. After a brief examination of the contents of the first box, I opened the second box. The box literally overflowed with cash. At the bottom of the stack, was yet another deposit slip. It was different from all of the other slips, so I look at it closely. It was a deposit slip for gold currency and the total amount was $38, 700. I stared at my grandmother in shock.

"Granny, where did you get all of this money?"

"The checks you sent...I never used any of the money. I was able to manage without it thanks to your Uncle J.T. and your cousin Lenny. Between the cash and the gold, you have a total of about $81,700 depending on the most recent cost of gold. The cost of gold back in 1993 was $371 per ounce, but it's declined a bit since then. Last time I checked, the price was around $248 an ounce. So far, the return on the gold is around $11,000, but it wouldn't be a bad idea to go ahead and sell it, if you like."

"Wait a minute, Granny, how did you become such a gold expert?"

"Something my daddy taught me years ago. He used to say gold is just like land--ain't nobody making any more of it. I took heed to his words. Whenever I get a few extra dollars, I use it to purchase a few ounces here and there. Been doing it over thirty years or better."

"I don't know what to say..."

"Don't say anything. The money is yours. Take it and put it to good use."

"That's exactly what I plan to do. Thank you, Granny."

"You're welcome, baby."

Chapter Seventeen
Halfway to Freedom

Amina and I reported to the halfway house the next day without a minute to spare. The St. Francis House was located just east of downtown New Orleans and only a few blocks away from the hustle and bustle of Bourbon Street. At first glance, it didn't seem like the best location for a group of ex-cons, but oh well.

After saying another round of good-byes, we were greeted at the front door by a female guard who waved a metal detector with one hand and held a breathalyzer with the other. We handed over our bags and proceeded to the bathroom for a urine drug test. We returned to find all of our clothes and personal items on the floor.

"They're clean," the lead guard announced.

While the atmosphere was less restrictive than our previous residence, the structure was pretty much identical. "Hall monitors" replaced the roaming prison guards, but their duties were the same. Their job was to maintain order and discipline, and based on my initial impression, they had their hands full. The ladies were sectioned off into groups. If I had to guess, the groups were compiled according to personality: the pretty girl group, the tough girl group, and of course, the lesbian group. This was very much like the prison environment -- same whore, different dress.

After the grand tour, we were taken to our rooms and provided with yet another list of do's and don'ts. By the time we were finished, we had ten minutes to make it to the cafeteria for breakfast. Neither of us were in the mood to eat and socialize with strangers. We decided to chill and wait for the orientation class that was right after breakfast.

"So, what do you think, Dana?"

"After six years in the federal pen, I can do this with my eyes closed. Twenty-nine days and a wake up."

"Word. I was thinking the same thing. So what's the plan?"

"We do the three days on lock, and then we hit the street. We gotta find a studio and come up with some beats."

"That's what's up. I can't wait to get my hands on a microphone. I can't believe this is finally happening."

We unpacked our belongings and headed over to the multi-purpose room for the orientation class.

"Glad you could join us, ladies. From now on, I expect you to be on time and not a minute late."

I looked at the clock on the wall and compared it to my watch. There was a one minute difference in the times. I took off my watch and set it five minutes earlier than the clock on the wall. I was not about to lose any privileges over something as petty as a one minute difference in the time. The orientation class was just a review of the information that we received in our transitional packets. It was basically a waste of time. I tuned her out after the first five minutes. I was thinking about the money that I had access to, compliments of my grandmother. Just like that, all of my immediate problems were solved. It meant I wouldn't have to ask Alex or my cousin, Lenny, for the money that we would need to pay for studio time.

"Ms. Toussaint, did you hear me?"

"Ma'am, uh...no, I didn't hear the question?"

"It's your turn to introduce yourself to the group. Tell us a little about yourself."

"I'm Dana Toussaint. I just finished a six year sentence in the federal pen for drug trafficking," I said slowly, looking around the room.

It would have been nice to hear what some of the other ladies had to say. I didn't see any shocked looks coming my way, so I figured I hadn't said anything that they hadn't already heard.

The next lady stood up and introduced herself.

I'm Kala Fitzpatrick. I just did a ten year bid for armed robbery. My kids needed milk and I needed another fix. I gave up ten years of my life, but I gained my sobriety. It was worth every minute."

Come to find out, Kala was a middle-aged White lady who had a thing for crystal meth. Her youngest child was born with special needs due to her addiction. All of her kids were grown now, and thankfully, her family was able to give them all a good home and keep them out of the system.

After Kala finished, there were only five ladies left to give their introductions. Each of the five that remained were fresh out of prison after doing time for various drug related charges. I wasn't surprised one bit.

After the orientation class, we were instructed to spend the rest of the day reviewing the newspaper for job opportunities. Next was dinner, followed by an evening group session. The evening session began with another round-robin discussion. We had to verbalize our goals for "becoming positive contributors to society." This time I paid attention and I have to say, it was quite entertaining. Most of the comments were extremely far-fetched, to say the least. For instance, the possibility of a thirty year old ex-junky becoming a runway model may be remotely feasible under the right circumstances, but a full set of teeth would be highly recommended. Justine was a beautiful girl, but years of drug abuse and fast living was visibly apparent. A chick named Carla wanted to become a law enforcement officer. I wasn't sure how that one would work out either, since she was completing a three-year bid as a repeat offender for mail fraud and forgery. Like the majority of the residents, drug abuse was the primary reason for their crimes.

Amina and I were prepared for this discussion and decided early on not to disclose or discuss any of our real plans. Our default responses were vague when the counselor asked.

"I'm planning to join my uncle in his janitorial business and possibly branch out on my own."

My response couldn't have been further from the truth, but it sounded good and it served its purpose. She moved on to the next person and I let out a quiet sigh of relief. Two more days of this and Amina and I would be free to hit the street.

Day number four couldn't have come at a better time. By then, I'd lost all of my patience with the monotonous day-to-day routine. We were up and dressed long before any of the other girls. We went over some leads we'd gotten from this one chick who claimed to know a few people in the music business. We weren't really sure if her information was legit, but we figured it was worth a try.

After hitting up just about every spot on our list without any luck, we were both frustrated and wondered if our goals were just as far-fetched as some other the other ladies'. However, on the last stop of the day, our luck changed. We'd saved this spot for last because it was the closest to the halfway house. It was apparent from the moment we entered the building that we were in the right place. The office was professional in a primitive sort of way and they even had a receptionist posted up in the front lobby of the small space to greet us. The other "studios" were the complete opposite.

"How can we help you?"

The receptionist asked her question with a friendly smile.

"We're looking for someone by the name of "J". We heard he was in the beat-making business," Amina stuttered.

"So, you're interested in possibly purchasing beats...am I correct?"

I could tell she was trying to get her point across up front. They probably had tons of drop-in traffic looking for a free hook-ups.

"Absolutely. We're looking to purchase some beats for a project we're working on."

I spoke up with a cool smile to let her know that her point was well taken--no freebies. Of course, that was fine with me. Money was not a problem. As a matter of fact, I appreciated the directness.

"Not a problem. Have a seat," she said and disappeared.

She returned a few minutes later with another pleasant smile.

"Right this way, please."

"What's happenin', ladies?"

Mr. J-Street greeted us with a warm golden smile and a thick South Louisiana accent when we walked into his office. His grille must have cost him a fortune and from the looks of his studio, he could afford it. I was no expert, but at first glance, the studio was state of the art. Amina was about to come unglued just at the sight of the equipment.

"I'm about to kick you a sixteen-bar. I'm looking for something really dope", Amina said.

She wasted no time spitting the sixteen for her favorite song. When she was done, J-Street went to his computer and presented three different beats. Each beat was fresher than the previous one.

Amina's eyes literally danced and she let out a sigh of relief.

"This is the spot, Dana. It's on."

Behind Closed Doors: *Dana's Story*

She was right. The beats were off the chain. We were running out of time, but Amina was able to give him a dry run of all seven of the songs that she wanted to use for her demo, and J-Street recorded each one. The plan was for him to provide two sample beats for each song and Amina would make her selections.

"Yo, these lyrics are tight, lil momma. Where you learn to flow like that?"

J-Street was totally digging Amina's sound and it wasn't a surprise. Amina was extremely gifted.

"It's in my blood and it's pumping and flowing, like a river full of pain 'cause I see awful thangs. But who am I to complain...?"

Her response was a bonafide free-style--another sixteen bar right off the top of her head. Little did she know, the verse would become the focal point for one of her greatest compositions.

Things began to come together nicely and faster than we anticipated. We left the halfway house each day under the guise of reporting to work with my uncle. In reality, we hung out at the studio and perfected Amina's sound. My uncle was a reluctant participant at first since I was being a little vague about my daily activities.

"Dana, you and your friend can come and work for me. I don't want you to make any bad decisions."

"Just trust me, Uncle Leonard. I swear, I'm not doing anything that will land me back in prison."

"Are you absolutely sure?"

"I swear."

He provided the necessary employment information to the clerk at the halfway house each week like clockwork and we just counted down the days. At the rate we were going, the entire demo tape would be completed by the end of our thirty days.

Mack and the kids were frequent visitors at the halfway house. Although my grandmother had decided not to visit me there, she made sure that Amina and I had a home cooked meal every weekend. I was completely okay with that and I understood.

Chapter Eighteen
The Transition

A few days before our release from the halfway house, I got a call from Tyree. As expected, he came with a list of lame excuses. It took a lot of doing, but I played it cool and just listened.

"Yo, Dee, it wasn't supposed to go down like that, I swear."

"Yeah, well, it did, but it's all good. I charged it to the game. That's how it goes, right?"

"I knew you were a ride or die from the moment I met you, Dee."

"Yeah...a true ride or die; that's me."

I clinched my fists so hard that I almost broke the skin. I wanted to let him have it right then and there, but there would be plenty of time for that.

"What about Ladasia? I'm sure you heard what happened."

Ladasia gave me the scoop on how things actually went down, but out of curiosity, I wanted to hear his side of things.

"I knew she wasn't built for a twenty-year bid, but I didn't think she would take herself out."

Tyree hesitated before he spoke.

"Drugs happened to Ladasia. It's really messed up how she went down but she did it to herself. After she started hitting the pipe, she just lost it. Unnecessary risk-taking is what landed her in jail. She just wouldn't listen."

Funny, he completely left out the part about her need to hit the pipe in order to lose weight--for him. What did I ever see in this man? He basically played me like he played all of his other women, and I bought it.

"So, why didn't you come to see me? Or better yet, why didn't you try to see your son?"

"I wanted to Dana, but I couldn't make it happen. You know, the wife and all."

"But, he's your son. He needed you, Tyree, and you just left him hanging."

"I did, but it's not what you think, Dana. I wanted to reach out to him, but it was too complicated. One day, I'll explain it all to you. For now, I just want you to know that I'm glad you're home."

He's glad I'm home. That's it. No "thank you's" for not snitching on his ass or "I'm sorries" for the fact that I have a criminal record that will follow me for the rest of my life. He made this revenge thing sweeter with each passing moment. Enough was enough. It was time for me to start spinning my web.

"Tyree, you owe me and I don't have to give you a list of reasons why."

"I swear Dana, I'm sorry. How can I make this right?"

He sounded sincere, but my mind flooded with images of Ladasia and thoughts of how he left me and Little Ty hanging for six years.

"I need to see you, Dana," he continued impatiently.

"What about your wife? I don't think she'd approve of that."

"Let me worry about her."

Wow. This man was a piece of work. The nerve of him to think that we could just pick up where we left off.

"I don't know, Tyree. I need to think about it. I have about a week left in this joint. I'll hit you up when I get home."

"Bet."

After I replayed the conversation over and over again in my head, I decided to call my friend Mellow to see what was up in East Boogie.

"What's good, homie? This is Dana."

"Yo, Dee, what's up? I thought you forgot about your boy."

"Never that. Got a few days left in this halfway house and then I'm good. What's popping in East Boogie?"

"Nothing much changed on this end. Same shit, different day."

"Who's running the streets these days?"

"Your boy Tyree and Mr. James got the whole city on lock. Seems they joined forces."

"Mr. James and Tyree?"

"Yep. All of the small time dealers packed up and bounced. Guess the body count got to 'em."

"You gotta be kidding me, Mellow."

Tyree actually had the audacity to try and hook up with me and he was rolling with my worst enemy.

"Anything else I need to know about?"

"You talk to your pops lately?"

"Yeah, we talk every day. Why, what's up?"

"I heard your girl, Miss Cookie, is kicking it with your pops in Florida."

"No way. She's my mother's best friend," I replied quickly.

Then again, the thought did cross my mind. Miss Cookie was hanging pretty tight with my dad during my brief moment of freedom at Granny's. In a way, I didn't know how to feel about this. She literally saved my life. If this was true, it meant she also betrayed my mother. Yet another shocking piece of information to digest. Betrayal was obviously the order of the day. Whatever happened to the concept of loyalty and boundaries?

"So, when you coming this way, Dee?"

"Soon. I still have a few days left in this joint and then I can move around. I need to check on my mom."

"Not a bad idea, Dana. Your mom is in bad shape."

"I figured as much."

To be honest, I didn't think I'd ever see her alive again. It was one of my greatest fears. The thought of getting the horrible news of her death was always on the forefront of my mind. There were so many things I wanted to say to her and so many unanswered questions.

"Oh, I almost forgot. What's up with the three amigos?"

They had to pay for what they did to Ja'El and their days were numbered.

"Same old thing -- still gettin' high and in and out of jail for petty crime. You know the deal. Not many H junkies left in East Boogie, but there's enough of them to warrant a steady supply through the city. Your boy Tyree and Mr. James are holding it down."

"Unbelievable."

Not only had he destroyed my life, Tyree was now my mother's dealer.

"Look, get at me when you touch down. Been hittin' the gym pretty hard. Think you'll be pleasantly surprised. By the way, I'm glad I took your advice. Balling is still my calling, but I'm doing it the right way."

I had to smile. Mellow still had a thing for me after all these years. He still wasn't my type, but it was good to know that I had a positive impact on at least one person in my life. Mellow was the proud owner of the most popular barbershop in the city. True to his word, he was balling out of control--with a pair of clippers.

"Absolutely, Mellow...Peace."

Chapter Nineteen
Revisiting the Past

It was time for me to face the one thing I dreaded most--my mother. After I spent a couple of weeks of uninterrupted time with my boys and the rest of my family, Mack and I hit the highway. I was really nervous about going back to East Boogie, but it was one of those things that just couldn't be avoided. Besides, my purpose for going was actually two-fold. I had to make things right for Ja'El. I felt responsible for what happened to her. Money was the main objective for the murders and I made her a target when I introduced her to the strip club. Even worse, my mother orchestrated the whole thing.

My first stop was the projects. I wanted to visit Ja'El's grandmother. I knew she planned to move back to Mississippi, but there was a remote possibility that she still lived with her sister. Things were pretty much the same in East Boogie. I honestly couldn't identify one positive thing about the city. Everything seemed to move in slow motion. None of the businesses thrived and there were more boarded up buildings than I remembered.

I knocked on the door of the apartment where Mrs. Jenkins lived before I went off to Gretna. An elderly lady answered the door.

"Good evening, ma'am, I'm looking for Mrs. Jenkins. I'm an old friend of her granddaughter's."

"Yes, I remember you sweetie. You paid for Ja'El's funeral and had her put away real nice. Come on in."

"Is Mrs. Jenkins still here?"

My excitement was quickly dispelled by her response.

"Well, yes and no," she replied.

"I had to put my sister in a nursing home. They say she has dementia."

"Dementia?"

"Yes, dementia. She kept wondering off and I got to the point where I couldn't stop her anymore. I was afraid that something terrible might happen to her if I didn't put her somewhere safe. These kids around here ain't got no feelings. They'd rob and kill you for a quarter."

She was right. This was definitely not an ideal place for the elderly or small kids. I wondered if she lived alone. She answered the question before I could ask.

"At least, I have some company here at night. Ja'El's little brother lives here with me. He's the good one. He works the day shift over at the waste treatment plant. That other one is in and out of the penitentiary."

I recalled that Ja'El told me that her two younger brothers lived with their respective fathers. Their lives were spared because of this.

"My sister is in the nursing home. Ain't but one here in town and its absolutely horrible. Half the time there ain't enough people to take care of all the residents. I go over there as often as I can to make sure they're doing right by her. Go on over there and see her if you like. It might do her some good."

"Absolutely, I think we'll head over there now. It's on Jackson, right?"

"Yes, it's the first building on the left when you turn on the street."

"Well, it was nice seeing you again. Do you need anything? Any errands to run?'

"No, sweetie; I'm fine. It was real kind of you to stop by."

"Here's my number," I said and handed her a slip of paper.

"If you ever need anything, just call."

"I sure will, honey. Y'all take care."

The nursing home was far worse than she described. I couldn't understand how they managed to stay in business.

"Hi, I'm here to see Mrs. Jenkins."

I spoke to the receptionist who never bothered to look up. She was too busy painting her finger-nails to be bothered with professionalism. She blew on her freshly painted nail and flicked her hand to the right.

"Oh, she's on the south end of the building, room 127."

I forced myself to keep quiet. Mack grabbed my hand and pulled me down the hallway before I could give the young lady a piece of my mind. The door to Mrs. Jenkin's room was open. She sat in a rocking chair that faced the window.

"Mrs. Jenkins." I called her name softly so as not to startle her.

She didn't answer, so I walked over to where she sat and said her name again.

"Mrs. Jenkins, this is Dana."

"Dana?"

She looked up and grabbed my hand as she tried to get up.

"No, don't get up, Mrs. Jenkins. I just came by to check on you. Everything okay?"

"Well, I been waitin' on you and Ja'El to come get me. Where is Ja'El?"

My heart skipped a beat. How was I supposed to respond? I didn't know if I should tell her the truth and force her back into a short-lived reality or if I should just allow her to think or believe a lie.

"Uh...Mrs. Jenkins, she didn't come this time. She'll come by to see you another day."

The sudden excitement in her eyes was quickly replaced by dullness.

"Why don't you let me put some rollers in your hair, Mrs. Jenkins," I said to change the subject.

I noticed a bag of rollers and a comb on the dresser.

"That's a good idea," she responded.

I greased her scalp and rolled her hair. After that, we went for a walk outside. I figured the fresh air might do her some good. Thankfully, she didn't ask any more questions about Ja'El. It was lunchtime when we returned, so I walked her down to the dining room.

"I have to go now, Mrs. Jenkins, but I'll be back to see you again, okay?"

"Okay."

The visit confirmed what I already knew. I had to make things right. Just to see Ja'El's grandmother in that condition removed any doubt. It also made me think about something else.

Conditions like dementia and Alzheimer's were like double-edged swords. On the one hand, an individual is spared the pain of recalling tragic events that might have occurred in their lives. However, on the other hand, the ability to recall vital information for normal day-to-day activity is lost as well. I couldn't decide which situation was worse. Perhaps the development of the disease was some sort of natural defense mechanism that the body uses to shield certain individuals from the torture of reliving painful experiences. Heaven knows, if anyone needed a shield, it was Mrs. Jenkins.

"Are you okay?"

Mack could tell that I was shaken by the visit.

"No I'm not okay, Mack."

"I didn't think so."

"I feel responsible for all of this. She wanted a job at the strip club because of me. She became a target because me."

"Listen, baby, none of this is your fault. But I promise you, I'm going to take care of this before we leave, you understand?"

I nodded my head to indicate that I understood. I turned my head and tried desperately to hold back the tears.

We rode in silence for a while until I regained my composure. I also needed time to prepare myself for what was about to transpire. I had the directions to the place where my mother was currently living thanks to Mellow.

"Dana, be careful. That place is crawling with desperate fiends."

"I know, Mellow. I'm good. I'm coming by the shop a little later."

"Cool. I'll be here."

The little house was located in the absolute worst part of town. It was daylight, so movement on the street was minimal. These people were your proverbial night owls. The kind that only came out at night. Mack took my hand and squeezed.

"You ready?"

"About as ready as I'll ever be."

"Let's go."

I didn't bother to knock on the door. I figured no one would answer.

"Hello," I whispered loudly and followed Mack into the dilapidated house.

"Diana Toussaint? Are you here?"

"Who wants to know?"

The response came from behind us. When I turned around, I realized it was my mother. She stood in the doorway.

"It's me, Momma--It's Dana."

"What the hell you doing here? Last I heard, you were still in the pen."

"I've been out for a while now."

Her indifference to my misfortune hurt a little more than I anticipated, which surprised me. She never bothered to hide her feelings in the past, so why would I expect anything to be different now?

"Can I talk to you for a moment? In private?"

I asked my question quietly and looked around the dimly lit room.

"Ain't nobody here, but me. Say what you gotta say and say it fast. I got things to do."

It was probably time for another fix, I thought.

Mack checked the only other room to make sure my mother told the truth. When he was satisfied that no one else was there, he stepped outside.

"Momma, I need you to tell me why..."

"Is that what you came here for?"

"Yes."

She looked me directly in the eye for the first time in years. For a moment, I thought she would apologize. I was wrong.

"I made some mistakes, Dana. Look at me," she said.

She slowly turned around so that I could fully examine her appearance.

"As you can see, I'm paying for it."

It wasn't an apology, but she finally conceded to the fact that she was wrong. She quickly changed the subject.

"So, your daddy and Cookie finally tied the knot."

"Not to my knowledge, who told you that?"

"Oh, I know everything. I ain't surprised one bit. That hussy was always jealous of me and I knew she had a thing for Bernard."

"When did you find out?"

"I suspected it years ago. As long as your father kept me straight, I just didn't give a damn. By the time I came to my senses, it was a done deal."

"I'm confused. You still hung out with her after Daddy left. If you knew they had something going on, why didn't you just cut her off?"

"Well, she never admitted to it, but a woman always knows, Dana. After your father left, I just pretended it never happened."

None of it made any sense. Who in their right mind would remain friends with someone who supposedly had an affair with their husband? It just didn't add up.

"Momma, do you believe in voodoo?"

"What the hell does that have to do with anything?"

"Nothing, I suppose. I was just asking..."

"I don't believe in any of that backwoods stuff," she said and cut me off. "And I don't wanna talk about it."

I could tell she was almost out of patience. If I was ever going to find out the truth about what she did to me and my father, it was now or never.

"I just have one more question. Well, two more questions. Did you and Mr. James...?"

"Don't ask me shit about Mr. James. He is the reason I'm in the shape I'm in now. The sick bastard deliberately turned me against your daddy by telling me about all the women your daddy was supposedly had. And I fell for it, Dana, hook, line, and sinker. All the while, he had his eyes on you, but I couldn't see it until it was too late."

"But, how, Momma? How could you let him..."

"How? Really? Look around you, Dana. I'm a junkie. James did this to me. He turned me into a junkie because he wanted to have his way with my daughter, and I let him do it."

I had a few other questions about Mr. James, but I decided to leave it alone. I was almost out of time.

"We need to get you into rehab, Momma..."

"Rehab? You gotta be kidding me. You know how many times I've been to rehab?"

"No, how many?"

"Hell, I don't know either--too damn many to count."

"There are other places. What about methadone? Have you tried it?"

Behind Closed Doors: *Dana's Story*

"Look Dana, don't start coming around here talking about no damn rehab, because it doesn't work and methadone ain't nothing but another habit. Besides, why the hell do you care?"

"You're my mother. I'm supposed to care."

"Well, since you care so damn much, give me some money."

So much for having a productive conversation with my mother. This one was definitely headed south. She couldn't even wait for me to leave before she pulled out her equipment and prepared her fix. When I left, she was huddled in a corner searching for a vein. I couldn't bear to watch.

"Come back here Dana!"

She screamed viciously when she realized I was leaving. "You're gonna just leave without handing me something? Come back here you little tramp."

She was right. Why should I care? I suppose its human nature, but people like my mother were incapable of such a thing. I gave it my best shot. If and when anything happened to her, my conscience was clear.

Our next stop was Mellow's barbershop.

"Yo, Dee! Good to see you, girl."

"Good to see you too, Mellow. This is my friend that I told you about. He wants to talk to you, privately."

Mack was determined to keep me out of the loop on this one. After all, I was the one with the prison record. Things could go bad really fast and he wanted my hands to be as clean as possible.

I stayed in the car. The conversation appeared to be going well. After the handshake and fist bump, I knew we were in business. Mack returned to the car and drove us in the direction of the bridge.

"I'm taking you across the river to the hotel, Dana. We have a little something worked out. It's going down in a couple of hours. That's all you need to know for now."

I was okay with that. I trusted Mack's judgment. A little time alone would be good. I had a lot to think about.

"Please be careful, Mack."

"All the time. I love you, Dana."

"I love you, too."

After a couple of glasses of wine, I was out like a light. Mack woke me up around midnight to tell me that the mission was accomplished.

"It's done, Dana."

"You gotta be kidding me."

I sat up in the bed and turned on the light so that I could see his facial expressions.

"About something like this--no. I made you a promise and I'm a man of my word. They'll never hurt anyone else."

"Did you get them to talk?"

"Yes, and that was the interesting part. I'll put it to you like this, Dana, heroin is absolutely *the* worst kind of addiction I've ever seen. I wouldn't wish it on my worst enemy".

Mack paused for a moment and gave me the rest of the details.

"One of them seemed to have a conscience. He said that he stayed high in order to keep Ja'El out of his mind. When he wasn't high, images of her were in constant rotation and permanently embedded in his mind. He actually asked me to take his life. He said he didn't deserve to live."

"Was he the one that..."

"No. One of the other guys was the rapist and he displayed no signs of remorse."

"Did they confirm my mother's involvement?"

"Yes. Apparently, she thought your friend stashed money in the house. They didn't find a single dime."

"The money wasn't there to begin with, Mack. It was at Miss Cookie's."

"I sort of figured as much. That's enough for tonight, Dana. Let's get some sleep."

"But Mack, I..."

"I know, Dana. I'll give you the rest in the morning."

"Really? You expect me to just go to sleep?"

"Yes."

I knew I wouldn't get any sleep, but I decided to at least give it a shot. The next morning, we were at breakfast when the news reporter provided the answers that Mack had been unwilling to provide.

"Two dead bodies were found in an abandoned building in the hillside area of East St Louis in what appears to be a drug overdose. The bodies were discovered by the owner of the abandoned building, who was contacted by an anonymous caller regarding suspicious activity around his property. The two victims were found with needles in their arms and syringes partially filled with lethal doses of heroin. According to preliminary reports from the coroner's office, the heroin was nearly one hundred percent pure. Antonio Watkins and Omar Harrison were known repeat offenders with extensive arrest records dating back to the mid-90's. Harris is survived by a wife and a teenaged son. Authorities are unable to locate the next of kin for Mr. Watkins."

"Mack, can you please tell me what happened? How did you manage to pull it off? And what happened to the third guy?"

"That's a good question Dana. Finish your breakfast and go back to the room. I'll be back".

Finish my breakfast? Really? When there was a junkie running around East Boogie with a story to tell? I could just see it now, 'ex-con and her boyfriend arrested for conspiracy to commit murder'. Unbelievable. I wanted to call Mellow, but thought better of it. No sense getting him caught in the middle of this mess. I went back to our hotel room, turned on the television and just waited. At some point, I must have fallen to sleep. When I woke up, Mack was there with a smile on his face.

"It's all good Dana. You have nothing to worry about."

"Can you please tell me what happened?"

"The other guy was located shortly after the news report. From the looks of it, he was smart enough to wait for the other two clowns to take the first plunge. When he saw what happened to them he decided to leave. He took the dope with him, thinking his friends mistakenly took too much. Seems he tried to readjust the dosage, but he didn't factor in the ninety percent purity. Apparently, he miscalculated the dose. They found him at a dope house around the corner from your mother. Thankfully, he was too selfish to share".

"Okay, go back to the beginning. Tell me what happened last night. How did you get all of them together in one place at the same time?"

"It wasn't hard at all. Junkies with habits like theirs will do anything for their next fix. They went to the abandoned building to cop some stolen goods. Your friend arranged it for me. By the way, Mellow is a real cool brother. I like the way he processes information without asking too many question. Just one problem...I think he still has a thing for you. He gave me his blessing though and a little warning. He said if I messed over you, he would take care of it personally."

The conversation must have been quite amusing because Mack was grinning, but I didn't see a damn thing funny.

"Okay, so what happened next?" My irritation was growing rather quickly.

"Once they were in the building, I made them sit in a corner and we spent the next few hours watching the clock. I knew it wouldn't take long for the withdrawal pains to kick in. When it happened, they started singing like a bunch of canaries. Once all of my questions were answered, I left. Apparently, they found the bag of dope that was on the table."

So basically, Mack's hands were clean...well, sort of clean. They injected themselves.

"But who called the owner of the building? Do you think anyone saw you..."

"No one saw me, Dana. I was the anonymous caller."

Chapter Twenty
Homecoming 1999

Alex

Dana was finally free after six years of incarceration. To top it all off, she came home to both her sons and a man who really loved her regardless of her flaws. In comparison, my personal life was still a mess in spite of my flourishing career and all of my accomplishments. My life basically revolved around my son, Jordan, and my career. The challenges of being a single mother overwhelmed me at times, but I was determined to do my best. Lawrence and I were "co-parenting" from a distance and any optimism about the relationship was long gone. I finally accepted the fact that our time had come and gone. At first, I was angry and bitter over the way things turned out, and of course, I blamed him. With the help of my therapist, Dr. Summers, I managed to get past those feelings and finally had a more positive outlook. However, in the back of my mind, I still wondered how I would feel if and when Lawrence began to date someone else. Dr. Summers and I were still working on that particular issue. Hopefully, it would be resolved before it actually happened.

I was enroute to GSU's last homecoming game of the millennium and Dana was meeting me there. I was a ball of nerves by the time my plane landed at the little regional airport that was a few miles east of campus. My arrival time was slightly earlier than Dana's, so I picked up the rental car and had a couple of drinks just to kill time. This year's game was going to be epic, I thought, as I took note of the massive number of GSU t-shirts I'd seen at the airport. By the time I finally spotted Dana, I had no less than twenty party invites for the weekend.

"Dana! Over here!"

I screamed above the loud noise.

"Girl, do you see all of these people? What the hell?"

Her eyes bulged with excitement.

"I know, right? I'm glad we decided to make the trip. Let's go!"

"Ok, tell me again how you managed to get a hotel for this weekend?"

I raised my eyebrow and laughed.

"I know people, Dana."

It hadn't been an easy task. The attendance for this year's game would more than exceed the accommodation capability for the surrounding areas. I called in a few favors through some long-standing connections in the area and they came through for me.

We made a pit stop at the hotel to freshen up and drop off our luggage before we made a beeline to "the yard." It was still early so we decided to kick it for a while before we checked out the storage facility where Dana's things had been stashed for the last six years. Before we knew it, it was almost five pm. The storage facility would have to wait until Sunday morning. We decided to follow the pedestrian crowd toward the village for a few pieces of Tasty's chicken for old time's sake. The route to the village was one that we knew well, and we both got a case of the giggles when we approached Que hill. Just like a scene from a movie or a recurring dream, Greyhound and Dee-dawg stood in almost the exact location where they stood almost ten years ago. Dana and I stopped in our tracks as the two men approached us. Ken was still breathtakingly handsome, but for some reason, it was more profound. Time served him well.

"Oh my God...Dee-dawg!"

Dana looked like she'd seen a ghost.

"Yes, it's me in the flesh. What's up Dana?"

He grabbed Dana in a bear hug. She laughed when he put her down.

"Oh, a little of this, a little of that...you know, grown folks stuff."

"Word?"

The two drifted away in deep conversation.

"Alexandra Phillips. Where the hell have you been? You know, I've attended every homecoming game since I graduated hoping to run into you."

"Oh, come on, Ken. There's no need to run game..."

"I'm as serious as a heart attack right now, Alex," he said.

"Wow. So, what's up with that?"

All of a sudden, I felt the nervous excitement. Truth be told, he was still a fixture in my mind as well. One of those "I wonder if..." sort of things. I fell for him for superficial reasons, but the thing that impressed me the most about Ken was his incredible kindness and maturity. I was just a kid, and he knew I was in way over my head, but he never attempted to take advantage of the situation. I was devastated when I didn't hear from him again. I finally chalked it up to the fact that he just wasn't attracted to me.

"Before we go any further, I need your phone number and a number for your next of kin."

"Ken, stop."

I was amused and flattered by his assertiveness.

"Give me your phone and let me dial the number."

He quickly handed over his cell phone.

"Done," I said and quickly returned his phone while I searched for mine in my purse.

"This is your number, right?"

I showed him the missed call on my phone. He nodded and grinned.

"So, how have you been Alex? What have you been up to all of these years? It's like you just fell off the face of the earth."

"Where do I start? Army, law school...life. And, I have a two year old son."

"Wow, you've been busy. I'm proud of you. For a moment there, I thought you were gonna tell me you were too busy to settle down. Wishful thinking, I suppose. Is he here with you?"

"Who, my son?"

"No, your husband. Did he come with you?"

"I'm not married," I said.

I pointed to my empty ring finger as proof.

"So, you're divorced?"

"Neither."

"I'm sorry, Alex, I just assumed..."

"I know, you assumed I was married because I have a two year old," I said and shrugged. "For some reason, marriage has eluded me. I'm a single mother."

He looked genuinely embarrassed about his assumption. I took pity on him and changed the subject.

"Enough about me. How about you? Wife, job, 2.5 kids?"

"No, not quite. I'm divorced. I have a 10 year old son and I own my own business."

"Sorry to hear that...the divorce, I mean, not your son."

What the hell was her problem? Who in their right mind would let this man get away? Not only was he breathtakingly gorgeous with his beautiful cocoa brown skin and perfect white teeth, he was obviously successful. I couldn't help but notice the vintage submariner Rolex he sported.

"Oh, don't be. We realized our mistake early on. No hard feelings between us."

"Ok, I gotta ask. What happened?"

"We weren't soul mates. I loved her, but it wasn't the kind of love that would sustain a sixty-year relationship. It just didn't work out."

Dana and Dee-dog headed back our way still in deep conversation. I had another flashback from our first day at Gretna. The weekend was becoming more and more interesting by the second.

"So, what do you guys have planned for the weekend?" Dee-dawg asked.

"No real plans. We're just gonna hang out and see what happens," I said quickly.

"In that case, here's two tickets to the Que party tomorrow night."

"Wow, we heard the party was sold out," I said as excitement rushed through my veins.

"It is, but you and Dana are officially on the VIP list," Dee said.

He handed the coveted tickets over to Dana. Like always, the Que party was definitely the place to be.

"Get there early before the youngsters."

Dana and I eagerly agreed. I remembered some of the Que parties that I attended back in the day. I had a feeling this one would be one to remember.

"I think we better get moving if we're gonna get anything to eat," I suggested to Dana.

I wondered if she and I were on the same page. There was the remote possibility that she might have other ideas regarding the way we spent the rest of the evening. I was wrong.

"Yeah, you're right," Dana said. "Nothing like being next in line when the grill shuts down. It was great to see you again Dee, and you too, Ken. It's been way too long."

"Yes, it has Dana. Get there early tomorrow night," Ken said with his eyes on me.

The chemistry between us was undeniable and it was totally different from the past. Was this even possible and if so why now? My life was a complicated mess and quite honestly, I didn't think I was ready for anything new as far as dating and relationships were concerned. I decided not to read too much into Ken's enthusiasm about seeing me. For all I knew, he could be the exact opposite of what he appeared to be. The potential was definitely there, I thought.

We made it to the village just in time. The chicken was just as I remembered--mounds of Tasty's special seasoning and just the right amount of grease to add to the flavor. From there, we made our way back to Greek row and kicked it with my sorority sisters for the rest of the evening. Surprisingly, all of my line sisters were present and we had a ball as we reminisced and caught up with each other. Dana and I finally headed back to the hotel around two a.m. to catch a few hours of sleep before the parade and the big game. Just as my head hit the pillow, my phone rang. It was Ken.

"Alex, I need to see you."

"Ken, it's nearly three in the morning."

"I know, Alex. Just come outside for a moment. I'm right out front."

"This is crazy. You know that, right?"

How did he even know where we were staying?

"Yes. I know."

I sat up in the bed and looked over at Dana who was curled up in the other bed and already snoring loudly. I started to wake her up to get her take on the situation, but decided against it. One of us needed a good night's rest. I threw on some sweats and a t-shirt, then grabbed my coat. Ken was parked out front in a dark colored

Range Rover. He immediately got out and opened the door for me. I crossed my arms and shook my head at him.

"Ken, this is crazy."

"I know, but I couldn't stop thinking about you."

"This better be good..."

He cut me off t before I could finish my sentence. His lips were as soft as I imagined ten years ago.

"Get in Alex," he said.

My heart pounded and followed his command. We rode in silence for a few minutes while a familiar jazz tune played softly. The name of the song was "Sunshine" by a popular Chicago band called Jabon. I was extremely impressed by his musical selection. I had an opportunity to see the band's live performance at the New Orleans Jazz Festival and they nearly stole the show from some other the other main stream acts.

"Are you planning to tell me what this is about?"

I whispered my question when the song came to an end.

"Absolutely."

He steered the truck down a hidden secluded road. I had to smile because as hidden as it was, it was a very popular little spot back in the day. Nothing changed. The place was just as beautiful as I remembered--open skies, trees, darkness and silence.

"I wanted you to see something," he said and reached into his glove compartment.

He held a photo of me asleep on his bed on that faithful night ten years ago.

"Oh my God, Ken. When did you take this? I had no idea..."

"Of course you didn't. You were asleep. I just couldn't resist. To answer your question, I'm not a psychopath. I felt something that night Alex and it was something that I never felt before. As you probably already know, I wasn't a saint back then. As much as I was attracted to you, I had no desire to take advantage of the situation, and believe me, the thought definitely crossed my mind. At first, I thought I was slipping, but I realized what was happening. You were special and I couldn't figure out why."

I wanted to say something but I decided keep quiet and listen.

"I wanted to contact you or say something to you every time I saw you on campus, but I was afraid."

"Afraid of what?"

"Afraid of you. I wasn't ready to feel what I felt and I wasn't in a position to really act on it. So, I just admired you from a distance."

"Wow, that's really deep, Ken. I felt something for you too, but I figured there was no sense in acknowledging it. You were an upperclassman, and I assumed you had enough women to occupy your time."

"Well, you were partially correct. I had a girlfriend, but the relationship was on the rocks when I met you. A few days after my encounter with you, I found out she was pregnant, so my experience with you became a moot issue. However, for the life of me, I could not get you out of my mind."

I was speechless to hear of his fascination with me.

"All of a sudden, we were planning a wedding. Her mother was absolutely livid about the pregnancy and wanted the wedding to take place as soon as possible. My parents weren't very happy about it either, but they wanted me to do the right thing. It was your typical shotgun wedding and the primary goal was to save face for her family."

I knew all about shotgun weddings. I was a catalyst to one myself. My mother was in high school when she got pregnant with me. She and my father were married in November and I was born in January.

"Like I told you earlier, I loved her, but I wasn't in love with her. Forgive me for using the cliché, but that's exactly how I felt. We graduated that December and had our son in April."

"How long were you married?"

"Two years."

Silence again. I tried to process everything that he said and tried to read between the lines at the same time. Ken broke the silence.

"Tell me what you're thinking."

"Where do I begin? I mean, I'm not an expert when it comes to relationships. I haven't had a successful one yet. I hate to say it, but to be honest with you, I've lost my optimism for the entire concept."

"Come on Alex, you have to give me more than that."

For a moment, I almost told him everything-even the part about my cousin Keith. I was convinced that he was the root of all of my problems when it came to relationships. In the end, I decided against it.

"Ken, the only thing I can say with certainty is that I'm the common denominator. Either I'm horrible when it comes to the selection process or there's something wrong with me. I'm still trying to figure it out."

The beginning traces of the sun were absolutely beautiful, I thought, as I stared through the passenger window. I was completely submerged in my feelings and overcome with a terrible sense of loneliness that was painfully intense. After years and years of trying to convince myself that I was destined to be alone, I suddenly realized I'd been fooling myself.

"Or maybe you just haven't met the right man. Have you considered that?"

He slowly reached over and tilted my head toward him. Before I knew it, we embraced in another kiss. When the kiss finally ended, I gasped for air.

"Ken, you have no idea..."

"Then tell me," he said and effectively cut me off with another kiss before I could give him the list of reasons as to why I couldn't maintain a healthy relationship.

"I would love to, but I think we should probably head back to the hotel."

"Okay Alex," he said with a sigh. "You win--for now, but I'm not letting you get a way this time."

After another deep kiss and another round of hypoxia, Ken dropped me off at the hotel. Dana was still sound asleep, so I laid there and replayed the entire scene. Ken gave me butterflies and that was something I hadn't felt in years. As exciting as it was, I didn't know if I could handle another round of disappointment.

At some point I must have drifted off to sleep. A well-rested Dana awakened me. She was ready to get the party started.

Behind Closed Doors: *Dana's Story*

"Wake up Alex. We have to get moving if we're gonna get a decent spot for the parade."

I looked at the clock and it was 7 a.m. Really? For a split second, I thought about ditching the homecoming parade, but I looked at my friend and realized she was determined to re-capture some of the experiences she had been forced to leave behind. We only had two days to make it happen, so I decided to take one for the team.

"Okay, let's roll."

It took me less than thirty minutes to shower and get dressed. We got there in time to see the parade and to reconnect with some old friends. The homecoming game was everything. We demolished our rival team and the party went into overdrive. We kicked it a little after the game before we headed back to the hotel to get ready for the Que party. Surprisingly, Ken and I didn't cross paths at all that day, but he called just before we left the hotel.

"Hi, pretty lady."

"Hi, Ken. What's up?"

"Just making sure I'm going to see you tonight."

"We're headed that way."

"Cool. I'll see you then."

"Ken is sweating you pretty hard," Dana said when I hung up the phone.

"I know. I think I really like him."

"I was hoping you would say that."

Dana sighed with relief. I turned an incredulous look on her. She held up her hand and smiled.

"Listen Alex, we're not getting any younger. If you're feeling him, roll with it. Life is too short."

I nodded and smiled back at her.

"You're right. I'm just gonna roll with it."

When we reached the party, Ken was at the door waiting for me. Gone were the conservative slacks and Polo shirt. Ken was now sporting an old pair of Levis, complete with rips and tears, with a pair of gold combat boots and a purple Omega Psi Phi t-shirt. From the looks of it, Ken was the prototypical Omega man by day and Que dog at night. Just the thought of his transition made my heart skip a beat.

"What's up, Dana?"

Although he spoke directly to Dana, he checked me out from head to toe. I was torn about my wardrobe for the evening, but from the looks of it I made the right choice. I decided to wear my hip-hugging low rider jeans with a cute little baby doll tee, in my sorority colors of course. As an afterthought, I wore my favorite pink leather blazer just to dress it up a bit. The blazer was custom made with subtle hints of apple green stitching.

"You look great, Alex."

"So do you," I said.

"Would you care to dance?"

"Sure, why not?"

The evening was unforgettable. Ken and I danced and stole kisses from each other so much during the evening that we were completely oblivious to everything except each other. I felt a little guilty about leaving Dana to herself, but she was having as much fun as I was, minus the stolen kisses. She made it clear to Dee-dawg that she wasn't interested in an encore performance from their previous encounter. He was cool with that. Her actions convinced me once and for all that her relationship with Mack was pretty serious.

The party finally ended around 4 a.m. When it was time to go, Ken insisted that I ride with him back to the hotel, which I did without hesitation. Dana and Dee-dawg followed suit in the rental car.

"So, what do we do now, Ken?"

"We follow our hearts."

"It sounds good, but I can think of at least three reasons why it would never work."

"Okay, I'm listening."

"You live in Atlanta and I live in D.C. I'm a single mother with "baby-momma" issues. Those two alone are enough."

"You're right, we have a few issues to address. Most of it is logistics. The important thing is that we found each other again. Everything else is secondary."

"What about my son's father?"

"What about him?"

"Our relationship is strange. It's like we're together, but we're not together. I can't really explain it. Whenever I try to define our relationship, it leads to an argument. I've even tried suggesting that we focus on co-parenting and put an end to the delusion. His response is always the same. He swears there's someone else, but there isn't. I'm just tired of the long distance relationship and I'm tired of playing house whenever it's convenient for him. I'm ready to move on."

"Are you sure you're ready to move on?"

"Yes, I'm sure," I said after taking a few seconds to really evaluate my feelings.

Who was I kidding? I wanted a real relationship and I felt like I deserved to have one.

"Then, that's what you need to do. Whether it's with me or someone else, you deserve to be happy, Alex."

We said our good-byes and made plans to meet at the airport the next day before Dana and I departed.

"Sweet dreams, Alex. I'll see you tomorrow."

"Good night, Ken."

Chapter Twenty-One
No Justice, No Peace

Dana and I woke up the next morning and replayed the events from the previous night. The entire experience was surreal-like freshman year all over again. Before we knew it, it was time to check out of the hotel and head over to the storage facility to sort through Dana's things. She brought an extra suitcase with her from home to collect the things she wanted to take immediately. She planned to return at a later date for the rest. The attendant escorted us to the correct location. Before he turned to leave, the shady-looking guy gave us a toothless grin.

"I've been working here for over twenty years and this is the first time I've ever had a customer to pay for as long as you did. The payments usually stop coming in after the first year or so. Once that happens, the contents are all mine. I figured there must be something pretty special in there."

The attendant obviously got a kick out of "confiscating" other people's possessions. Placing that particular account on auto-draft was the smartest thing that I ever did. His comments seemed to rattle Dana a bit as well. She rolled her eyes, but managed to hold her tongue.

"I know exactly how many boxes I have, Alex," she whispered as the attendant hobbled back to the main office.

"If even one of 'em is missing, it's going down."

I said a little prayer before I handed over the set of keys, which had been in my possession for the last six years. I knew that Dana would have no trouble keeping her word if anything was missing.

After we struggled with the rusted and worn padlock for a few minutes, we finally managed to open the door. All of Dana's things were just where I'd left them. She methodically opened each and every box and selected the items that she wanted to take with her. When she got to the last box, she hesitated for a moment and gave me a strange look. She took a deep breath and slowly began to open the box. Buried beneath several layers of clothing, was an orange and white shoebox. When she opened it, hundred dollar bills began to spill all over the place.

"Dana, do you mean to tell me..."

"Alex, I can't believe that it's all here...all of it."

"Exactly how much is 'all of it', Dana."

She counted the money several times before she revealed the amount.

"Fifty G's."

"Damn!"

I screamed and jumped around the cramped space like a little kid.

"Dana, this was a gangster move, for real."

"I know," she said.

"I honestly didn't know if the money would still be here or not. I prepared myself for the worst."

"What you did was sheer genius. I assumed all of your money was in the bank."

"Never put all your eggs in one basket, Alex. Tyree was extremely generous to me at first. I figured the money train would end or take another route at some point, so I started to stash money early in the game."

"Brilliant. So what are you planning to do with the money, Dana? Whatever it is, it's gotta be good."

"I know. Trust me, it won't go to waste. I have a plan--a legal plan. I didn't do these six years for nothing. Believe that."

Dana managed to get all of her flyest gear into the oversized suitcase along with the shoebox filled with money. On the way out, she told the attendant

"It's all yours, I won't be coming back."

From a legal standpoint, transportation of that amount of money on a plane was out of the question. We made the split second decision to extend the car rental and drive to New Orleans instead. However, not before I had a chance to say good-bye to Ken. He was parked at the Denny's directly across from the tiny little airport as planned. Dana went inside for two large coffees, and I hopped into the truck with Ken. Very few words were exchanged because they weren't needed. After a series of long passionate kisses, I glanced through the rear-view window. Dana frantically made her way toward Ken's truck with her cell phone up to her ear. Her facial expressions suggested something very serious was happening on the other end of the phone.

"Alex, you have to come to Memphis with me. Amina's little brother was just shot by the police. They don't think he's going to make it."

"Tell her we're on our way," I said.

My heart raced and the hair literally stood up on my skin.

The country as a whole experienced an overall reduction in crime and violent activity in the late nineties and the economy thrived under the leadership of President Clinton. The statistics confirmed my personal views concerning crime and poverty. The two issues were intricately linked and tied together. Dire economic circumstances are precursors to crime and violence and the city of Memphis was a prime example. Plagued with the unrelenting consequences of poverty, Memphis was at the top of the list for crime and violence when compared to other impoverished communities with similar demographics. Substandard education and the lack of opportunities for economic growth were the contributing factors.

If the rest of the country was thriving, why were cities like Memphis, Detroit, and East St Louis still struggling? On the surface, this type of contradictory information would lead one to postulate an abundance of negative theories about these and other cities with similar demographics. Images of Black on Black crime propagated by the media, further added to the negativity. In reality, the average American was unaware of the fact that the country was undergoing a rigorous change in policing strategies in order to combat the proliferation of urban violence. However, the issue of poverty remained unchecked. The new crime fighting approach included the use of profiling techniques and an increase in the use of technology for the surveillance of high crime areas. Overall, the changes did little to curtail the violence and crime within the urban community. A degree in rocket science was not required to understand the fact that failure to address the poverty issue would negate or seriously minimize any efforts to eradicate crime and violence in the inner-city. In the meantime, reports of police brutality and the senseless killing of young Black men by the police were at an all-time high. I was willing to bet this case would be no different.

According to Dana, Amina's family left the fast pace life of New York and returned home to Memphis with the belief that the smaller city would provide a better environment for their children. Sadly, this would not be the case. They'd already lost one child to the allures of the Memphis streets, which resulted in a lengthy jail sentence, and they were now faced with the potential loss of another child at the hands of the Memphis police.

Timothy was a good kid who had the misfortune of being born with a disability. Autism is a developmental disability that causes significant social, cognitive, and behavioral challenges. On the outside, individuals with autism appear to be no different from anyone else. However, their interaction with others and their behavior is altered and they learn in ways that are different from most other people. Amina's mother went through great lengths to raise her son to be independent and self-sufficient. She even battled with the Shelby County school board to create a sufficient learning environment for Timothy and kids like him. Timothy graduated high school the previous year and was the proud owner of a small lawn service. Because of his inability to drive or operate a vehicle, his customers were required to have their own lawn equipment and Timothy provided the labor. Timothy's business took off rather quickly due to his kind and gentle demeanor, and the power of positive word-of-mouth advertisement. He was on his way home from work when he was suddenly stopped by a couple of Memphis cops who were patrolling the neighborhood. According to the officers, Timothy was "acting suspiciously" and fit the description of a robbery suspect. He was gunned down for failure to comply with the universal command, "put your hands up."

Ken graciously volunteered to drive us to Memphis. We returned the rental car and after a quick word of prayer from Ken, we were on the road headed north on Highway 167. Dana received a few calls from Amina along the way, and from what I could gather, things were not looking good. The three hundred mile journey was extremely quiet and solemn with each of us lost in our own feelings concerning the situation. I was extremely thankful that Ken and I shared the same tastes for music. The smooth sounds of

Jabon played softly through the speakers and provided a perfect contrast for the apprehension and melancholic mood that we all experienced.

We only made one stop, which was at the half way point, in Pinebluff, Arkansas. Ken got us to Memphis in record time. We reached the hospital just as the family exited the building and my heart sank. Sadness and pain was written on each of their faces.

"He's gone, Dana," Amina whispered, "they killed my little brother over a damn cell phone."

Amina sobbed uncontrollably along with the rest of her family. Her father stood silent and tried desperately to control his anger as he came to terms with the harsh reality.

"I'm so sorry, Amina," Dana said, as she hugged Amina.

"This is my friend, Alex, the attorney. Tell us exactly what happened. She may be able to help."

"Hi, Alex."

"Hi, Amina. I'm so glad to finally meet you. I just hate that it had to be under these circumstances. Tell me what happened."

Amina took a deep breath and recounted the events.

"It happened right around the corner from our house. Timothy was walking home from work when two policemen decided that he looked like the suspect involved in a series of burglaries in the area. When they approached Timothy, he didn't hear what they were saying because he was wearing headphones and listening to music. As Timothy removed the headphones, his cell phone began to ring. When he reached for the phone, one of the cops opened fire. They killed him over a cell phone, Dana," Amina repeated.

She was in tears again. She and Timothy were really close. She'd always been his protector and now her worst nightmare had become a reality.

I heard all I needed to hear and I seethed with anger. Someone had some explaining to do. We followed Amina to her parent's house. After consulting with her parents, I made a call to the police station and demanded to speak to the Chief of Police. They gave me the run around for a few minutes, before he finally took my call.

"Ma'am, this matter is settled..."

"So, that's what you're going with?"

I cut him off before he could finish his sentence. I was not in the mood for any default commentary. I wanted answers.

"Just who do you think you are to talk to me that way? If you want a discussion, you need to start by speaking respectfully."

"Fine, have it your way, Chief."

Alex must have had all of the local media outlets on speed dial. Within a matter of minutes, she'd arranged a press conference at the courthouse. The family was in no shape to attend, so Alex, Ken, and Dana would go alone.

"Mrs. Jackson, I can't bring your son back, but justice will be served. I promise."

"Thank you, baby. Do what you can," Mrs. Jackson said before they left.

The news crews were already gathered outside the police station when they arrived. Alex went straight for the small makeshift podium that was provided by one of the news crews.

"An autistic child lost his life today in a manner that is absolutely unfathomable. Releasing her child to the world, outside of the realm of her protection, has always been his mother's greatest fear. Timothy Jackson was determined to beat the odds and he was well on his way to doing just that. In spite of his disability, this child had his own business. As a matter of fact, he was on the way home from work when he was gunned down. According to the trigger-happy policeman who fired the fatal shot, Timothy was stopped because he fit the description of a burglary suspect. Here's a photo of the real suspect...and here's a photo of Timothy. No resemblance. The police chief has informed me that the preliminary investigation for this case is already complete and that the officer acted appropriately. I have a serious problem with this and so does Timothy's family. I want this case re-opened immediately and I am calling for an internal investigation to determine why the case was closed with such rapidity. I want answers. And above all, I want this officer's badge."

The crowd erupted with applause as cries of "no justice, no peace..."rapidly spread.

The city of Memphis was no stranger to the ramifications of civil and social injustice. In addition to its festering socioeconomic issues, Memphis was also the place where Dr. Martin Luther King met his untimely and devastating demise. After Dr. King's death, riots quickly spread throughout the city of Memphis and 4,000 National Guard troops were eventually ordered into the city. One wrong move and the city could find itself in a similar predicament, reminiscent of the one that occurred in the Spring of 1968.

In light of the mounting tension within the community concerning Timothy's death, the police chief reluctantly made his way to the podium to follow Alex's impromptu press conference. Before he presented his rebuttal statement, the chief looked into the crowd and found Alex. The color visibly drained from his face as he stood there and conceded to the fact that this woman had somehow forced him into the checkmate position.

"My condolences to the Jackson family on the loss of their son. As the Chief of Police, my job is to ensure that each and every facet of the law is upheld and that justice always prevails. As a result, this case has been re-opened. I urge you to take Officer Bryant's record as a veteran police officer and his selfless service to the city of Memphis into consideration along with all of the mitigating circumstances that pertain to this case."

"Chief, can you offer any explanation for the brevity of your preliminary investigation?"

The reporter must have read my mind. It would be impossible to conduct an impartial investigation in less than twenty-four hours.

"I'm not at liberty to discuss any details regarding the case at this time..."

"Are your officers adequately trained in the appropriate use of force?"

Another reported chimed in.

"No further questions," the chief said.

He retreated to the safety of his office as the crowd resumed their chants, "no justice, no peace."

Alex was at the police station bright and early the next morning and Ken was by her side. While Alex was consumed with the task of ensuring justice for Timothy's family, Ken was just as consumed with ensuring Alex's safety. The situation in Memphis was volatile to say the least, as protestors continued their peaceful demonstrations around the city. Not only did she provide legal oversight for the family, she also played a key role in maintaining the peace within the community. Her daily appearances on the local news and gentle pleas for protestors to "allow the system to work" seemed to have a calming effect on the Memphis residents. Hopefully, her pleas for optimism would not be in vain and justice would be served.

Ken contacted his office to let them know that he would be out of pocket for the rest of the week. Alex and Dana shared a hotel room and Ken was just across the hall. Because Dana spent most of her time with Amina's family, Alex and Ken had plenty of time to themselves.

"Alex, I'm impressed."

"Thanks, Ken, but would you care to elaborate?"

"Your confidence and your tenacity--you're fearless."

"You think so?'

"Absolutely. I'm making a mental note to never cross Alexandra Phillips."

"Okay, you made your point," Alex said, completely amused by Ken's assessment.

"I think I missed my calling. I toyed with the idea of becoming a civil rights attorney, but I let my professor talk me out of it. He said I'd never make any money if I went that route. I take on these type of cases whenever I can just to make up for it."

"Again, I'm impressed."

"Thanks, Ken."

"So, what's next with the case?"

"According to the officer, Timothy appeared to be "high" at the time of the incident. The internal affairs officer had to wait for the findings from the toxicology report before he could render the final decision. The report came back today and contrary to the officer's claim, Timothy wasn't high on anything except the prescription eye drops he used to treat a mild case of glaucoma. I'm expecting a press conference no later than tomorrow afternoon. The officers involved in the shooting are on paid administrative leave, pending the official announcement of the internal affairs investigation. Oh, and the trigger happy cop decided to get ghost. He packed up his family and moved back to Arkansas."

"So what do you think will happen to him? Could he receive criminal charges?"

"Not likely, but I'm determined to push the issue as far as I can. The number of "justifiable homicides" by police officers far exceed the number of officers who are charged with murder or manslaughter in cases like these. But one thing is for sure, this guy will never work in law enforcement again."

Timothy's funeral took place the following Saturday, six days after the senseless killing. The family was still overcome with grief, in spite of the investigation being ruled in their favor. The officer who took Timothy's life was fired and criminal charges were pending. I had first-hand knowledge of the pain associated with this type of loss and the grieving process. A multi-million dollar settlement was sure to come, but no amount of money could ever repair the damage.

Dana

Amina took the loss of her brother really hard and for a while it seemed she would never regain her passion for music or anything else for that matter. As a result, our plans were at a complete standstill. I finally got a call from her about a month after her brother's death.

"Book me some studio time. I gotta get this off my chest."

She arrived in New Orleans the next day and J-Street was ready for her. Somehow, he managed to get an internationally known underground artist to do the hook for the song and it was completely off the chain. As Amina stood in front of the mic, I could see the passion in her eyes and I could also feel her pain as she recited the lyrics to the song "No Justice No Peace". She was back. Ironically, a portion of the sixteen bar freestyle that she recited for J-Street during their initial meeting, was the most captivating part of the song:

"It's in my blood and it's pumping and flowing,
Like a river full of pain, 'cause I've seen awful things;
But who am I to complain, about the inconsistencies and
the wanna-be's, trapping us daily, modern day slavery,
No justice, no peace, how can my brother RIP and his

killer walk free? Is there a heaven for a "G"?
I hope one day I'll get to see, until then, I will hold my peace..."

Amina's lyrics were filled with gut-wrenching reality and everyone in the room could feel it. There was complete silence when she finished the recording.

"That's a wrap, Lil Momma."

J-Street was the one who finally broke the silence. The song was completed in just one take.

Chapter Twenty-Two
Confirmation

Composing the "No Justice, No Peace" track was therapeutic for Amina and she was finally back in the studio to put the finishing touches on the demo. Music became her refuge as she slowly came to terms with the loss of her brother. She stayed in Memphis long enough to make sure that her family was okay and now, she was ready to grind.

Since I had some free time on my hands until the demo was complete, I figured it was a good time for me to take a trip to Florida to see my dad. I was proud of my father for the way he'd turned his life around. He'd joined my uncle's practice as the chief administrator in charge of personnel and all business related activities. My uncle finally had someone that he could trust to run his practice and was now free to practice medicine without the added stress of dealing with non-clinical issues.

This would be my first trip to Florida since I was a little girl and I was excited to visit with the other side of my family. However, this was not a vacation. It was time for me to have a heart to heart conversation with my father. I needed him to confirm some of the things that Tyree shared with me when we first met. I also had a growing list of questions that needed answers. At the top of the list was my mother and her relationship with Miss Cookie. The conversation I had with Ms. Angélique concerning my mother's condition was still fresh in my mind,

"*Someone put a root on your mother, Dana,*" Miss Angélique said, "*and I'm sorry to tell you, it's the worst I've ever seen.*"

"But who would do such a thing, Miss Angélique?"

"*We may never know the answer to that question, Dana. It had to be someone very, very close to her.*"

Although I wasn't completely sold on the voodoo theory, it was something to consider. I was eternally grateful to Miss Cookie because she took in, but was my father the ulterior motive? Had she done something to cause my mother's demise in order to finagle her way into my father's life? If this was truly the case, then Miss Cookie was partially responsible for all of the horrible things that happened to me. The whole scenario was a bit far-fetched and I conceded to the fact that I was probably searching for a reason to justify my mother's actions toward me.

Aside from the personal issues, I also wanted my father's account of my mother's role in his incarceration. I needed all of the pieces to the puzzle before I could proceed with my plans. Thankfully, my father was alone when he picked me up from the airport. After we caught up a bit on our day-to-day lives, I got right down to business.

"So, Dad, what's the deal with mom and Miss Cookie? I gotta be honest, when I found out you were kicking it with her, it didn't sit well with me."

"I figured it wouldn't. That's why I kept it away from you for as long as I could. It's complicated, but it's not what you think. Cookie and I didn't hook up until after I went to jail. Prior to that, I couldn't stand her," he said with a little chuckle.

"Why didn't you like her?"

Interesting, I thought. After all, your first impression of a person is usually pretty accurate. Maybe she worked a little magic on my father as well.

"Nothing in particular. I just didn't want your mother to socialize with a bunch of single women. I figured she was a bad influence."

He paused for a second and seemed to struggle with whatever he had to say next.

"I blame myself for your mom's drug problem, Dana. I should have kept a closer eye on her."

"She's a grown woman. Unless you put the syringe in her hand or supplied the dope, I can't see how any of this is your fault," I said, trying to dispel any feelings of guilt my father might carry. My mother was a junkie because of her own choices.

"It's not that simple, Dana. Your mother was a little "out there" when I met her. I knew she was trouble from day one, but I fell in love with her the moment I set eyes on her. Looking back, all of the signs were there."

"What signs?"

"She had what I would call an addictive personality. I can't really put it into words, but it was as if she was trying to lose herself

Behind Closed Doors: *Dana's Story*

in something. Whether it was booze or weed, it didn't really matter to her. I thought if I could remove her from her environment, she would be free of whatever troubled her. I was wrong."

Wow. I knew where my father was going with this information. My mother obviously had some type of traumatic experience as a child. I recalled something that my grandmother said about my mother's rebellious behavior. These were all signs of abuse, but who was the abuser?

"Moving to East St Louis was the biggest mistake I ever made in my life. Crack was the drug of choice when we got there, but heroin was still pretty popular at the time. I think your mother's curiosity got the best of her. Long story short Dana, I placed her in an environment that she was not equipped to handle. Therefore, I have to take some of the blame."

"Okay, I hear what you're saying, but what does any of this have to do with Miss Cookie?"

My mother was a heroin addict, but that alone did not justify Miss Cookie's betrayal.

"Cookie and I didn't start to communicate until I got wind of what was going on with your mother and Mr. James."

"So, you're telling me that Miss Cookie knew about Mr. James?"

"No, not everything. She was under the impression that Mr. James was responsible for you working down at the strip club-- which is what I thought as well. We had no idea that your mother was actually..."

He couldn't bring himself to say the words. It was just as well. I didn't think I could stand to hear him say it.

"So, anyway, I contacted Miss Cookie and asked her to keep an eye on you. A few days later, I found out that you were living with her. So, I hate to use the cliché, Dana, but it's true. It just happened."

"She was my mother's best friend."

"I know, Dana. She's not proud of the way things happened, but I can assure you, it wasn't deliberate. It just happened."

"I guess I have to trust your judgment on this one, but, Dad, if I ever find out that she's not the person you think she is, it won't be pretty."

I was surprised by my father's reaction to my dramatic declaration. He laughed out loud and couldn't seem to stop.

"What's so funny?"

I was annoyed. Apparently, he thought I was playing.

"I'm sorry, dear. I don't mean to make fun. It's just that you remind me of some of the women back home. The fiery spirit is definitely hereditary."

"Yes, it is, but I meant every word."

"I know, Dana."

"Just one more thing. Was my mother really involved in your arrest?"

"Yes, she was."

I knew it was a touchy subject. The anguish at the mere mention of it was all over his face.

"That was by far the worst day of my life," my father's accent grew thicker with raw emotion, "and not just because I'd been caught. I was hurt because I knew that your mother was involved."

"Absolutely. I had an uneasy feeling that night, so I changed the drop location several times. Right before I left the house, I instructed your mother to dial a phone number at precisely 8:15 pm and to simply read the address to whoever answered the phone. The person on the other end of the phone had nothing to do with the operation. It was just a random number."

"Why would you have her call a random number?"

"The uneasy feeling lead me to do it. It was a huge risk, but I was testing your mother's loyalty. As it turns out, I was right. Your mother followed my instructions, but she made some additional calls as well. The cops were there before I could even step out of the car and James was right behind them."

"She set you up," I whispered and tried to visualize the whole scene.

"She called James and James called his buddies from the police force. Thankfully, the greedy bastards took enough of the merchandise to keep me from getting a life sentence. I had twelve kilos of coke on me at the time, but somehow, only three kilos made it to the precinct."

"Unbelievable."

"Yes, it is, but greed worked in my favor again. Because I was charged with just three kilos, I was able to bond out in less than twenty-four hours. The day of my last visit with you occurred just a few hours after my release. My lawyers were able to delay the case for over a year, and I sent child support payments like clockwork. Your mom's restraining order was the only thing that kept me from seeing you again"

"This is worse than I ever imagined. She wouldn't let you see your own children? How could she be so evil?'

"In hindsight, it was probably for the best. I might have ended up in jail on a murder charge if I came into contact with your mother or James. The judge allowed me to await my trial in Florida thanks to my brother."

We continued our journey in silence for a few minutes and then my father finally spoke,

"Some of the hardest lessons I've ever learned came from your mother, Dana.

"Same here."

Chapter Twenty-Three
Woman to Woman

The rest of the visit with my father was uneventful. Since he was convinced that Miss Cookie was the best thing that ever happened to him, I decided to respect his wishes and accept his decision to marry my mother's best friend. However, I still had my doubts. A real friend would never consider a relationship with her best friend's husband. My father was aware of my skepticism and so was Miss Cookie. The two of them would have to prove me wrong.

During my visit to Florida, I had plenty of time to think about my next move. I decided it was time to move forward with phase two of my plan. A conversation with Mrs. Carter was long overdue. On the evening of my return to New Orleans, I gave her a call.

"Mrs. Carter?"

I was startled when she answered the phone on the first ring.

"Yes, this is Mrs. Carter."

"This is Dana."

"Hmmm. I heard you were out, but I didn't expect to hear from you so soon."

"Really? And why is that?"

"I hoped that you'd learned your lesson. Seems the system failed to teach you the importance of respecting other people's boundaries."

Other people's boundaries... Her mouth and her attitude made it easier than I thought.

"Let me get something straight, Mrs. Carter. You're still married to a man who has cheated on you and disrespected you for years and you're calling me disrespectful?"

I never quite understood the concept of blaming the other woman for a husband's indiscretion.

"My husband is not a saint, but he's a wonderful father and provider. Unfortunately, he has a thing for trashy women."

"And you're okay with that? You're okay with the fact that your husband sells drugs to take care of his family?"

I decided to ignore the little insult. Mrs. Carter was in perpetual competition with God knows how many women and her husband was the prize. Her superiority complex was clearly a defense mechanism, but I was confused. Why would a self-sufficient, educated woman find contentment in a cheating husband who fathered a child outside of their marriage?

"I know what my husband does for a living. He doesn't force anyone to use drugs, he simply supplies a demand that was already in place. Look, I don't have to prove anything to you. You should know that my husband loves me. You spent six years in jail. If that isn't proof, I don't know what is."

That was the last straw. I spent six years in jail because of her lying-ass husband and she had the nerve to rub it in my face.

"So, my six years in jail is proof enough for you? What about all of the other women? Let me ask you something Mrs. Carter. Have you ever wondered how it would feel if the shoe was on the other foot? Can you imagine being away from your kids for six years? You're married to a drug dealer. One wrong move and you could find yourself in the same situation..."

"Are you threatening me?"

"No, sweetie. I'm offering you an opportunity to get out while you can. You see, I just recorded this entire conversation. You verbally acknowledged the fact that you are aware of your husband's occupation. You are, by your own admission, an accessory to the crime. In case you didn't know, to have knowledge of a crime before or after the fact is enough for a conviction."

"You bitch..."

"Call me whatever you wish, but here's the deal, I'm the bitch who stands between you and a prison cell. Tyree is going to pay for what he did to me and if you're smart, you'll make him pay for what he did to you. If you love him enough to sacrifice your children and your career, I have to respect that. However, you have options."

I waited in the tense silence for an answer.

"I'm in."

The reluctant reply was music to my ears.

"You're a smart lady, Mrs. Carter. Keep this little conversation to yourself. You'll hear from me soon."

Mission accomplished. Tyree's wife was extremely vital to the mission and to my surprise, it was much easier than I expected. I couldn't believe she actually fell for the tape recorder thing without asking for proof.

Chapter Twenty-Four
Retributive Justice or Revenge

So far, things were going according to plan, but a simple phone call from J-Street put us in overdrive.

"Dana, I got some good news for you."

"Cool, but you don't sound very excited about it. What's up?"

"Well, I know you guys already have plans your demo, but I did something that you may not approve of. I shared one of the singles with a couple of guys that I know in the industry without your permission. Long story short, two major record labels are ready to make you an offer."

"And you thought I wouldn't approve of this? Are you serious? This is much better than the prospect we had."

Truth be told, I wasn't even sure if Tyree had enough connections to make things happen for Amina. It was just a chance we were willing to take.

"Arrange the meeting."

"Done. I'll let you know as soon as I have all the details."

"Thanks for looking out. This is exactly what Amina's been waiting for—a real opportunity."

"She deserves it."

"Yes, she does."

Our original plan was to use Tyree's connections in the music industry to get Amina's career off the ground. We hoped our interactions would give us some inside information concerning Tyree's continued illegal activities. Thanks to J-Street, we no longer needed Tyree's services, and his days on the street as a free man were officially numbered.

The information that Ladasia shared with me along with my recent conversations with Mrs. Carter gave me a better understanding of the man who almost ruined my life. Ladasia told me that the Carter's were high school sweethearts and that Tyree began peddling dope in junior high. She was right. Although our situations were totally different, he had the means to rescue his wife from a bad situation just like he rescued me. According to Mrs. Carter, she was raised in a single parent home and things were really tough. Tyree's generosity made it easier for the whole family. That was the person she fell in love with, and the same was true for me.

Eventually, his predatory ways would overshadow his positive attributes. After high school, he encouraged her to attend college, and quite naturally, he was her primary means of financial support. This was almost identical to my own experience with Tyree. Somehow, her suspicions concerning Tyree's occupation and the source of his generosity weren't confirmed until her senior year in college. I found this a little hard to believe. Either she was extremely naive or she was blinded by love--or perhaps it was greed. By then, she was well on her way to becoming a commissioned officer in the military. Her immediate response was to end the relationship; however, she'd just discovered she was three months pregnant. Against her better judgement, she married Tyree with the condition that he would put an end to his criminal ways. When she realized he had no intention of holding up his end of the deal, she proceeded with her own career plans with the military. She knew that he would never leave Chicago, so she hoped that the distance would eventually allow her to sever the ties between them. Unfortunately, her plan didn't work. In the end, Tyree enjoyed the best of both worlds--a wife with a reputable career and a few side-pieces scattered across the mid-west. Over the years, she'd grown content with the lifestyle that he provided for her family, and she learned to live with his infidelity. However, when she found out about Little Ty, she was ready to give it all up. According to her, my six-year prison sentence was the only thing that "saved" her marriage and her home life improved tremendously after my arrest. However, it was short-lived.

"In case you didn't already know, Tyree didn't waste any time replacing you, Dana. And by the way, please call me Chantel."

I gave her a call a few days after our initial conversation and her attitude had improved tremendously.

"Cool. I was beginning to think you didn't have a first name," I said jokingly. "About Ladasia--yes, I knew about her. A friend of mine from East Boogie kept me up to date on the happenings. She basically followed in my footsteps. Don't tell me you were behind her incarceration as well. Did you hear what happened to her?"

"Yes, I heard what happened to her, but I had nothing to do with her incarceration. When I found out about her, I didn't even bother with the ultimatums. It was pointless. However, it made me realize my husband was never going to change",

"I'm confused. Tyree is a serial cheater; I wasn't the first and I'm pretty sure I wasn't the last. So, why me? How did I end up becoming the fall guy?"

"You were different. Out of all of the other women, you were the one that captured his heart. He was in love with you, so I had to do something."

She said it as if she were discussed the weather or the new Coach bag that she wanted to purchase. To her, I was an object or a thing, devoid of feelings or emotions. Sending me to jail was a temporary remedy for her situation, but it was pure hell for me. I was not surprised by her revelation, but hearing it straight from her heightened the intensity of my anger and disappointment in Tyree. As for his Chantel, I actually felt sorry for her. She too, was as much a victim as I was. Tyree was an insecure woman's worst nightmare. His ability to fix all of the things that were broken, while making you believe that you're the center of his universe, was more powerful than any drug. However, the gig was over. Our eyes were open and we were officially fed up.

"You know, Chantel, I dreamed of having this conversation with you every single day when I was locked up and I had a long list of things I wanted to say, but I don't think it's necessary at this point. We're in the same boat."

"So it seems. I think it's time we did something about it. What's the plan?"

"I need information--detailed information."

"Tyree has never discussed the business with me. However, I know enough to keep me one step ahead if anything ever went down."

"Okay, I'm listening."

"For starters, the Texas connection ended when you went to jail. Everything is moving out of Florida and headed straight for Louisiana via I-10."

Smart move, I thought.

"Before I go any further, I need you to help me understand something. You had enough information on Tyree to cut a deal. Why didn't you save yourself?"

"I didn't want my family to suffer for my mistakes. I could have gotten a year on probation in exchange for testifying against Tyree, but I was afraid that Tyree would use my family to get back at me. I just couldn't take the risk."

"Wow, and all this time I thought you did it because you loved him."

"Well, now you know."

"As I said, the route changed..."

As Chantel began to name the specific locations and other vital information, I was finally convinced that her efforts were sincere. She was fed up.

"I can always tell when a new shipment is coming through due to the change in Tyree's behavior."

"Are the shipments coming in weekly, bi-weekly...?"

"Twice a month."

"So, I have a question for you. If you're not getting this information from Tyree, where is it coming from?"

"I think I'll keep that to myself, Dana. It wouldn't be wise for me to reveal my source."

"As long as the information is accurate, I can live with that."

I laid out the preliminary plan for Chantel. The rest would have to be arranged.

****

We were in the midst of the holiday season. Like always, the depression began to surface. My boys were happy, Mack consistently amazed me and I was surrounded by the people who loved me. What more could I possibly ask for?

Suddenly the phone rang--it was Mack.

"Dana, I'm coming to pick you up. We're going for a ride."

There was a cool urgency in Mack's voice, but that was his style.

"I'll be ready when you get here."

Ten minutes later, he knocked on the door.

"That was fast. You must have been right around the corner."

"Something like that. You ready?"

"Yes, I'm ready. Where are we going?"

"Hold your horses, Lil Momma. I got a surprise for you."

We headed towards the West Bank, so I figured we were going to visit some of his friends in Marrero. We finally pulled into the driveway of a beautiful home in a gated community. I thought I knew all of Mack's friends, but apparently, I didn't. When we reached the door, he didn't knock. He pulled out a key and opened the door. Just inside the immaculate foyer, a banner hung from the ceiling, "The Bergerons." My knees began to shake as Mack reached out to grab me in his arms.

"Dana, will you marry me?"

I nearly fainted when I saw the beautiful princess cut diamond.

"What took you so long?"

My whisper echoed through the foyer.

"The house...I wanted to wait until it was finished. I built it just for you."

"Mack, it's beautiful, but I would have said yes even if we had to live under a bridge."

"I know, Dana. You deserve the world, and I plan to give it to you."

"I love you, too."

I hugged him and then pulled away to catch my breath. I didn't want to spoil the mood, but after his last comment, I knew it was time for me to voice my lingering concerns. For some strange reason, I was a magnet for men in the drug dealing profession. I couldn't imagine going back to prison on another drug charge and I refused to lose my husband to the penal system. I loved Mack, but I was prepared to walk away if I had to. Thankfully, I was in a position to support my family until Mack was able to settle on a different career path. I had my grandmother to thank for that. I also had the money from the storage unit. There was a little under over a hundred thousand dollars remaining, after the fees for Amina's studio time were paid. Half of the money would be set aside for the kids' college fund and the rest I planned to keep for a "rainy day". However, this was a sacrifice I was willing to make.

"Mack, I need to make something clear."

"I'm listening."

"I can't marry you if you're still hustling. I have enough money for us to live on until you find a job..."

"Dana, I stopped hustling a long time ago. Trust me, I can take care of my family."

He seemed quite amused by my suggestion.

"But what about the trucks...?"

I had assumed the fleet of eighteen wheelers were a front for some type of illegal activity. Apparently, I was wrong.

"Those trucks are legit, and so is my business. I would never risk being separated from you again. No matter what."

His words were music to my ears.

"There's one other thing..."

Since he was going to be my husband, I figured he should know about my plans for Tyree. I didn't leave anything out.

"Give me Chantel's number."

That was his only response.

Tyree was arrested three days later. Chantel came through like a champ with the information. The feds pulled Tyree's runner over when she crossed the Louisiana-Mississippi line. Chantel's prediction was dead on when she told me that the runner wouldn't hesitate to cut a deal with the police. She spilled the beans on the entire operation before she even reached the police station.

In the wake of the arrest, Chantel learned that Tyree had three other children.

"I'm so angry right now, Dana. He told me that your son was the only one. I can't believe he slept with all of those women without protection. I hate him, Dana..."

Tyree was sentenced to twenty years of hard labor in the most notorious prison in the country--Angola. He deserved every single minute of it.

I didn't ask Mack for any additional details. I trusted his judgment. In addition to his trucking business, Mack assumed all of the managerial responsibilities for Amina's budding career. In the meantime, I was busy planning our big day. I had exactly two months to make it happen and it had to be perfect. Alex was there every step of the way along with my sisters. My mother was the only missing link. I couldn't understand why it bothered me so much because she'd been absent from every other important event in my life.

Little Ty and Isaiah were excited about the new house and their relationship with Mack gave me a sense of peace. My sons entered this world with the cards stacked against them, but Mack and I were determined to even the playing field. Hustling and drug dealing would not become the default option for them. The cycle would finally be broken.

Behind Closed Doors: *Dana's Story*

Chapter Twenty-Five
Six Degrees of Separation

January 29, 2000 was the happiest day of my life. It was my wedding day. I woke up that morning with the kind of joy that I had never experienced, but I was still a little anxious. A little anxiety on your wedding day was generally expected, so I forced myself to focus on things that produced a minimal amount of stress. My bridal party allowed me do so. Alex and my sisters handled all of the last minute details and minor issues. The wedding was scheduled for five o'clock that evening, so I spent the entire day in the hands of people who were hired to make me "flawless."

My investment in the wedding planner was worth every penny and the wedding went off without a hitch. In hindsight, I had to admit I pushed every one of her buttons, and there were times when I thought she would offer me a refund. At the end of the day, I wouldn't have changed a thing.

The reception was held at the Ritz Carlton on Canal Street in the French quarter. The vintage fleet of beaming white Rolls Royce's that transported the bridal party and immediate family members to the hotel garnered an enormous amount of attention from onlookers along the route. The four-course meal, which included lobster and steak, along with the live jazz band solidified the first-class experience. Without a doubt, the Bergeron's were officially positioned among the New Orleans elite as they entered their realm of "happily ever after."

Alex

As Dana's maid of honor, my job was to facilitate the perfect execution of her fairytale wedding and I was determined to make it happen. I was up at six that morning for my scheduled hair and facial appointments. My next stop was the church for a last minute inspection. I was a little concerned about Dana's color scheme at first, but when I entered the sanctuary and saw the unique blend of antique gold and white with splashes of warm earth-toned colors, I was convinced she'd made the right choice. The color combination coupled with the rich interior of the church resulted in a perfect display of elegance and style. The champagne colored bridesmaid dresses would provide a perfect contrast.

The wedding began promptly at five o'clock. Dana's grandmother was the first to enter the church and she was absolutely beautiful in the champagne colored two-piece suit that she wore. Amina, Dominique, and Dahlia were next. The single strap ensembles were created by a local seamstress. The dresses were uniquely different and designed to accentuate the individual qualities for each of the ladies. As the maid of honor, my dress was slightly darker than the bridesmaids' dresses and the design was completely different. The V-neck halter gown was long and flowing with an exaggerated split in the front, which provided a tasteful display of my best feature--my legs. I was thoroughly pleased with the selection.

After the entrance of the bridal party, Little Ty and Isaiah escorted their mother to the halfway mark of the sanctuary, and her father escorted her the rest of the way. The gesture was a well-executed display of solidarity among the men who were most important in her life. At the rate that I was going, my make-up was going to be all over my dress from the continuous flow of tears. As I recounted the seemingly endless list of tragedies and adversities that Dana endured prior to this point in her life, I just couldn't help it. When I finally got a chance to scan the audience, I realized I wasn't the only one in tears. Tears of joy flowed all over the sanctuary.

As I looked around the room, my eyes fell on the last two people I would ever expect to see in the crowd. It was Lenny and Sierra. For the life of me, I couldn't put an end to the puzzling gaze that lingered between me and my cousin's husband. The dangerously uncomfortable feeling was still there and it disturbed me. Why was he there? What was the connection? I was literally lost in my feelings as I racked my brain to figure out the connection between Dana, Lenny, and Mack. There was a remote possibility that Sierra was the source of the connection, but it was unlikely. The soulful voice of the soloist finally put an end to the lingering gaze that Lenny and I shared. Mr. Clark was a well-known local musician and vocalist. He sang an old Al Green classic, *God Bless Our Love.* If you closed your eyes as you listened, you would have been convinced that Brother Al was actually in the building. The song was absolutely perfect for the occasion and Mr. Clark's rendition was simply amazing.

The remainder of the wedding was as beautiful as the beginning, but the reception was most definitely the icing on the cake. From the ride in the Rolls Royce, which Dana left as a surprise for all of us, to the red-carpet entrance into the Ritz Carlton, I was completely amazed by the alluring displays of beauty and the tasteful grandiosity. Although I'd never had the pleasure of being a bride, I considered myself a professional bride's maid due the number of weddings I had participated in over the years. Hands down, this was the most beautiful of them all.

From personal experience, men with commitment issues were usually a little reluctant to attend weddings. If this was true, Ken earned major points in the "keeper" category for his enthusiasm alone. Our relationship continued to grow by leaps and bounds, and I was finally able to embrace the possibility that "happily ever after" could still happen for me.

After a few dances with Ken, I found myself alone at the bar after he excused himself to the men's room. All of a sudden, Lenny stood right next to me. After a little chat, Lenny and I answered each other's questions as to our mutual presence at Dana's wedding. As it turned out, he and Dana were first cousins. In addition, Mack and Lenny were childhood friends. Once again, I had evidence to support the fact that we are all connected to some degree. However, the fact that Lenny and I actually shared multiple connections through a set of extremely unlikely circumstances made me wonder if there was some type of supernatural reason for it all.

"Why do we keep crossing paths, Lenny?"

"I'm wondering the same thing, Alex. So, how have you been?"

"I'm good. Think I finally figured this whole single-motherhood thing out."

"I can't believe you're still single. I had a brief conversation with your friend. He seems like a pretty decent guy."

"Is that so?"

So, Ken had Lenny's stamp of approval. I figured this was probably a good thing, but the complexity of the situation was something that I would have to explore with my shrink. Most likely, it was nothing more than physical attraction. Whatever the case, I needed to process my feelings for Lenny once and for all.

"He loves you, Alex. My instincts have never failed me when it comes to this sort of thing, and that's the vibe that I'm getting. Give it a chance. You deserve to have someone like him in your life. Your son's father is a serious piece of work. If he couldn't appreciate what he had in you, he doesn't deserve a place in your mind or your heart."

I didn't bother to say it, but he was absolutely right.

"By the way, I know what you're thinking, and it's okay. Listen, I love your cousin, and I'm happy. But, at the same time, I know in my heart that if you and I had crossed paths under different circumstances, things would have been a lot different. Do me a favor, and don't overthink it. Seize life and live it to the fullest. I could be wrong, but I don't think you've ever allowed yourself to do that. It's time that you did."

"Thanks, Lenny."

Perhaps I wouldn't need my shrink after all. What he said made perfect sense. The attraction between us was just that--an attraction. Thankfully, we never acted on it, so in reality, it meant nothing.

"No need to thank me, Alex."

Sierra and Ken showed up at the bar at the same time and we brought her up to speed.

"Wow Alex, I think I need a list of all of your friends. We have to stop meeting this way".

After catching up on things back home, we went our separate ways. Lenny was right. I had to let go so that I could move on. I contemplated Lenny's words for the rest of the evening.

During the last dance, Ken did something that totally took me by surprise. I would later discover that it was actually planned well in advance by Dana and Ken. As the music became softer, I looked around and noticed that we were alone on the dance floor. Ken lowered himself to one knee and took my hand.

"Alex, will you marry me?"

Chapter Twenty-Six
Dear Momma

Dana

I couldn't think of a better way to end the night. Alex was finally going to get a chance to walk down the aisle. The positive energy that flowed throughout the building screeched to a halt just as Mack and I prepared to make our final toast. My father pulled me to the side with a grim face.

"Dana, I just got some bad news."

Before my father even spoke the words, I knew he was going to tell me something horrible about my mother. What else could it be? Every important person in my life was in my presence with the exception of my mother.

"Your mother is in the hospital. They don't think she's going to make it."

In a matter of seconds, my entire evening was ruined. Instead of boarding a plane to Turks and Caicos the next morning, I was headed to East Boogie--a place that I had no desire to visit.

"I'm coming with you, Dana. I need to be there," my grandmother said.

My grandmother would never board a plane, so our travel options were limited. We quickly changed clothes and prepared for the pre-dawn six-hour road trip. My sisters and my brother were visibly shaken, but neither of them volunteered to accompany me on the trip. Although I understood their indifference to our mother, it was something that needed to be discussed. But it would have to wait.

"Dana, I'm coming with you," my father said.

I wanted to say yes, but I decided against it. I didn't think it was appropriate for Miss Cookie to be involved in whatever was going to unfold. I could tell that she was relieved when I said no.

"I'll be okay. I'll call you if I need you to come."

"Dana, Ken and I..."

"I know what you're going to say, Alex. The answer is no. I want you to enjoy the rest of your time here and I'll keep you up to date. It's a six-hour drive, Alex. Promise me you won't hop on a plane and beat me there."

It was exactly the kind of thing she would do.

"Ok, Dana," she said reluctantly. "Just let me know something as soon as you can."

The journey to the place that held so many bad memories for me was extremely long and restless. I couldn't get my mind to shut down enough for me to go to sleep. I think my grandmother experienced the same thing. To my surprise, she was awake for the entire length of the trip.

We finally arrived at the hospital at around eight in the morning and headed straight for the intensive care unit. Thankfully, we made it in time to speak directly to the doctor who was in charge of my mother's care.

"Her condition is extremely critical, but it's difficult to make an accurate prognosis at this time. Right now she's stable, but in the next few hours, things could change in either direction. It would be wise for you to consider your worst-case scenarios. Irreversible brain damage is pretty high on the list of concerns. In the event that Mrs. Toussaint fails to emerge from her comatose state, you'll need to indicate your wishes in regards to the type of long term care the family would desire. You'll also need to decide whether you'd like to execute a 'do not resuscitate' order."

"Who would be responsible for making those decisions?"

My grandmother must have read my mind. Clearly, neither of us wanted the ominous responsibility, but we had to be prepared.

"The immediate next of kin would make the final decision: husband, child, then parent."

My grandmother slowly sat down, and for the second time in my life, I listened to her cry. The night that my mother told us that she'd given Little Ty up for adoption was the first time.

"Visiting hours won't began until nine, but if you'd like, you can come with me."

None of us were prepared for what we saw. There were tubes everywhere and she was connected to a machine that breathed for her. Her skin was a horrible mess with track marks that covered every possible area of her body. Her hair was really the only recognizable thing on her body.

"Feel free to stay as long as you want."

The doctor was right. It didn't look good. He placed a hand on my grandmother's shoulder.

"I'll be around if you have any further questions."

The doctor left the room with a glance of sympathy. My grandmother nodded and placed a hand over her heart. She moved to the bed very slowly, as if her feet were heavy.

"How could you do this to yourself, Diana?"

My grandmother whispered tearfully as she stroked my mother's hair.

Mack and I left her alone with my mother. It was the first time she'd seen her daughter in almost eight years. I figured she could use the privacy. She joined us in the waiting room a few minutes later.

"It doesn't look good, Granny."

"I know, but I'm still praying for a miracle."

"We won't be able to visit again for a couple of hours. Let's get something to eat."

"No, you two go ahead. Just bring me something back, so I can take my medicine. If I take it on an empty stomach, I'll be sick as a dog."

"Got taste for anything in particular?"

"No, I don't have taste for much of anything right now. Whatever you bring is fine."

It was nearly ten by the time we left the hospital--too early for lunch and too late for breakfast at most of the restaurants in East Boogie. We decided to head over to the twenty-four hour Wal-Mart to see if we could find something in the deli.

"I better get some gas, Dana. We're running on fumes," Mack said and pulled into the convenience store.

Not that there were very many gas stations to choose from on that side of town, but I wished Mack had chosen a different one. This particular store had a recurring role in my worst dreams. It was the store where Mr. James took me to purchase my favorite candy and snacks.

When Mack went inside to pay for the gas, I let the window down for some fresh air. Suddenly, I heard a familiar voice.

"Dana."

Mr. James stood right next to the car. Fury burned, and then cooled in my veins.

"I can't believe you have the audacity to step to me after what you've done to my family. Were you the nice clean cut gentleman that dropped my mother off at the hospital?"

One of the nurses asked me if my father was still around to sign some admissions paperwork. Initially, I thought maybe my dad decided to make the trip against my wishes, but that would have been impossible. It had to be Mr. James.

"You should thank me for saving her life. When I found her she was barely breathing."

"Thanking you? Why should I thank the man who got her strung out in the first place?"

"I had nothing to do with that. She was a junkie long before I met her. Ask your daddy. Listen Dana, why don't you let me...?"

"Let you do what? After all these years, you're still a perverted bastard."

"But you liked it, Dana. Don't you remember how we used to..."

His words cut through me like a knife and before I knew it, I had Mack's .38 revolver in my left hand. Mack never left home without it.

"Come on Dana, stop acting like you don't remember."

"Step away from the car."

"I want you to come with me."

"I'm going to tell you one more time--step away from the car, James!"

What happened after that is quite simple. I snapped. When he suddenly reached inside of the car and attempted to touch my hair, I lost it. The bullet was lodged in the left side of his chest at close range. He hit the ground just as Mack exited the store.

"Dana, what happened?!"

I stood over Mr. James' as Mack made his way toward me and everything began to move in slow motion.

"I think I killed him, Mack. I killed Mr. James."

By then, I could hear the police sirens in the distance. Mack grabbed me and held on until they arrived.

"It's gonna take a while before they book me, so don't waste your time coming with me. Just go back to the hospital and tell my grandmother what happened."

Surprisingly, I was completely calm. The worst part about the situation was the impact it would have on my grandmother. Her daughter was in a coma and her granddaughter was probably going back to prison. The officer shook his head and immediately placed the handcuffs on me when I told him I was the shooter.

"I don't know what happened here, but I can tell you for sure, this guy wasn't worth it."

Apparently, the officer aware of Mr. James' status in the community. And he was right, Mr. James was not worth the trouble. However, if he and his colleagues would have done their job, I wouldn't have been forced to do it. I turned to look at Mack's grim face.

"Call Alex."

Chapter Twenty-Seven
Murder Was The Case

Mack went back to the hospital to break the news to my grandmother. She was pacing the floor when he walked into the lobby.

"Baby, where's Dana? Her mother just woke up and they're taking her off that breathing machine. It's a miracle."

"Mrs. Ledoux, sit down. I have something to tell you..."

Like always, my grandmother handled the devastating news like a champ.

"Lord, have mercy...if it ain't one thang, it's another. I don't know what's happening to my family. It was him, wasn't it?"

She clearly referred to Mr. James.

"Yes, ma'am."

"Well, he got what was coming to him. I just wish it would have been someone other than Dana. She's been through enough already. So, what are we gonna do?"

"I called Alex. She's on her way, and so is your son. Hopefully, Alex has a license to practice in Illinois. If not, she can at least point us in the right direction.

Alex

"What did you just say?"

I picked up the phone to call Dana when my cell phone rang.

"She killed him," Mack stated calmly.

"I went into the store to pay for gas and when I came back, he was on the ground in a pool of blood. He must have said something to her Alex. I'm planning to go back to the store to see if there were any surveillance cameras in the parking lot."

"Ok, where did she get the gun? She's a convicted felon. It's against the law for a convicted felon to handle a handgun."

"It was mine, Alex. The gun was in the car."

Dana had a mountain of cards stacked against her. For one, Illinois was not an open carry state. To handle a handgun without a permit was illegal. On top of that, she was a convicted felon with a drug charge. It was going to be hard to convince a jury that Dana was incapable of cold-blooded murder.

"I'm on my way."

Ken and I were on the next plane out of New Orleans accompanied by Dana's father, Miss Cookie, and Dana's Uncle Leonard--Lenny's father. The immediate family spent the night at the Ritz, so I was able to notify everyone at the same time. Dana's sisters didn't take the news well at all. They blamed their mother.

"I don't understand why she even bothered going down there in the first place. I can assure you that our mother wouldn't have returned the favor."

Dana's younger sister was clearly not at fan of her mother. The other sister was more concerned about Dana's chances to avoid to avoid another prison sentence.

"What are her chances, Alex? I'm trying to decide whether or not to tell the boys."

"Let's wait a few days before telling them. I need to see how serious the charges are before I can start building a case. After what he did to her, there has to be a way to get her out of this mess."

When I went to her father's room to break the news, he was already in a fit of rage. Dana had used her one phone call to call him. Lenny and his father were there along with Dana's uncle from Florida.

"I should have taken him out a long time ago. How the hell did this happen?"

Mr. Toussaint was out of control with anger.

"I don't have all of the details, but from what I've heard so far, we may have a viable case of self-defense. Beyond that, the only other option would be the 'crime of passion' defense. If we can get enough admissible evidence concerning the abuse, we may have a case."

"Exactly what type of lawyer are you, Alex? I know you're her friend, but Dana's going to need a damn good criminal defense attorney for this one."

Dana's uncle, the physician, was concerned about my ability to handle the case. Under the circumstances, I wasn't offended by his lack of confidence.

"Listen, I need everyone to calm down. If anyone can handle this for Dana, it's Alex. I've seen her in action."

Behind Closed Doors: *Dana's Story*

The vote of confidence from Lenny was enough for Dana's father, but I could tell her uncle was still a little skeptical.

"Sir, I handled a similar case a few years ago. The defendant faced a capital murder charge in Louisiana for killing her abuser. She was found not guilty."

Everything happened for a reason. I was convinced beyond a shadow of doubt that I found my purpose in life. Like Yasmine, Dana faced the prospect of going to prison because she committed a crime against her abuser. Yasmine and Dana were victims, and in my opinion, their actions were justified. Once again, I had to prove it.

Strangely enough, Illinois was one of first bar exams that I elected to take right out of law school. I chose Illinois for no specific reason at the time, I just thought it was a good idea to have a license in that particular state. Once again, my instincts served me well. As a result, I wouldn't have to deal with the complex reciprocity procedures and I could start representing Dana immediately.

We arrived in time for me to attend the arraignment with Dana. The purpose of the proceeding was for the defendant to hear the official charges and to determine whether or not a bond would be set. It was also the point at which Dana would give her official plea.

She was charged with second-degree murder and a felon in possession of a firearm. In Illinois, and most other states, felons were not allowed to handle or possess a firearm. The conviction for felon in possession was punishable by imprisonment for up to five years and a fine not to exceed $25,000.

Based on Dana's prior conviction and the felon in possession charge, I fully expected a first-degree murder charge from the prosecutor. Thankfully, I was wrong. In the state of Illinois, first-degree murder is usually charged when death occurs in conjunction with a forcible felony such as rape, aggravated burglary, or with premeditation. Second-degree murder, as defined by the state of Illinois, is the intentional killing of another person that occurs under sudden or intense passion from serious provocation by the individual killed without any planning or premeditation. The state of Illinois also takes into consideration certain mitigating circumstances, which may also result in the lessening of a charge from first-degree. However, the reduction of a first-degree murder charge to second-degree murder typically occurred after the preliminary investigation is complete--not before. In a case like this one, the more serious charge is usually presented at this stage. The early issuance of the second-degree charge at this point was a positive indicator for Dana. In my opinion, it was a subtle display of compassion on behalf of the prosecutor. Mr. James was definitely not a citizen in good standing, and I had a feeling that this was probably the sentiment shared by the community.

As it stood, Dana faced a conviction of second-degree murder, which carried a sentence of four to twenty years prison time in the state of Illinois. However, the judge also had the option to sentence Dana to four years of probation. The circumstances that surrounded the crime and the compassion or leniency of the judge would be the determining factors for whether she received prison time versus probation. With the right jury, there was also a possibility that she could be found not guilty.

In order to secure a conviction, the prosecution had to prove beyond reasonable doubt that the defendant knowingly and intentionally acted (without pre-meditation) in a manner that would result in death and that the defendant's actions were unjustified. Potential defenses for second-degree murder included among other things: insanity, lack of knowledge or intent, intoxication, and self-defense. In Dana's case, lack of intent and lack of knowledge were not viable options.

It would be impossible to prove that Dana was unaware of the fact that a bullet to the chest at close range would result in death. Without a doubt, her actions were intentional. Intoxication was out as well. Temporary insanity and self-defense were the only viable options. If the convenient store was equipped with security cameras, it might have captured the triggering event that preceded Dana's actions. This would prove that her actions were justified. If all else failed, I was prepared to go with the crime of passion/temporary insanity defense as the mitigating factor that caused Dana to take action. My job was to provide a preponderance of evidence to substantiate the mitigating circumstance for justification. Simply stated, I had to plant just a seed of reasonable doubt to obtain a verdict of 'not guilty'. However, the burden of proof beyond a shadow of doubt was required for a guilty verdict.

We had options. That was more than we could ask for under the circumstances.

The next order of business was the entrance of a plea. Dana indicated to me that her plan was to enter the *nolo contendere* or no contest plea. She was convinced that her prior criminal history would result in a maximum sentence and she was hesitant to roll the dice. The *nolo contendere* plea would allow her to accept punishment for the crime without admitting or denying guilt in the hopes to receive a lighter sentence from the judge.

"Absolutely not, Dana. We have a good case."

My words were not meant to foster false hope. I honestly believed we had a good case.

"Not guilty, Dana, just trust me."

"Not guilty."

Dana's reply was slow, but I think she realized it was the right thing to do.

The bond was set at $100,000 which meant she would be going home with us. It also meant that we would have one hundred and sixty days to prepare for trial. Defendants who are denied bail are required to appear in court within one hundred and twenty days which is in accordance with the individual's constitutional right to a speedy trial. We needed as much time as we could get for a couple of reasons. For one, it would give Dana more time to spend with her family and it would give me some extra time to prepare her defense. Dana was released and given permission to await her trial in Louisiana.

"Looks like you better start to plan that wedding, Alex. I know you think I have a good case, but this thing could go either way. I want to be a bridesmaid before I'm fifty."

We left the courthouse and headed to the hospital to see Diana. Apparently, she'd defied the laws of karma once again and was on her way to a miraculous recovery. Dana and I entered the room first. Diana was no longer in the intensive care unit, so there were fewer restrictions on visitation. To our surprise, she sat in a bedside chair with an untouched tray of pureed fruit and a glass of water. Somewhere underneath the years of bad living was a very beautiful woman. Dana warned me about the ugly track marks that covered her body, but they were concealed by the long-sleeved pajama set that Diana wore.

"Momma? It's me, Dana."

"I know who you are, and I heard what happened. Did you really have to go and kill him, Dana? With James out of the picture, there ain't nothing moving through East Boogie. The junkies gonna be dropping like flies around here. People like you would never understand this monkey we got on our backs. We don't shoot dope because it makes us high. We shoot dope because it keeps us from being sick enough to die--or wishing we were dead."

I found it more than a little disgusting that Dana's mother would choose to discuss the state of narcotic trafficking in East St. Louis at a time like this. Her daughter had just been charged with second-degree murder of the man who not only stole her childhood, but also sent her father to prison and turned her mother into a junkie. Dana didn't appear to be phased by her mother's inappropriate reaction at all, but I had a few choice words on the tip of my tongue. Somehow, I managed to keep my thoughts to myself.

"Listen, I'll leave the two of you alone. I have some calls to make and this may be a good time for me to go and take a look at the crime scene."

The tension in the room was too thick and Diana's attitude was under my skin.

"Thanks, Alex."

"No worries; I'll be back in a few."

Dana

"Momma, I may need your help."

I forced herself to say the words for fear of my mother's reaction. My instincts were correct.

"I hope you don't think I'm gonna help you get out of this mess. How the hell am I supposed to help you? I can't even help myself."

"I may need you to testify..."

"Are you crazy?"

My mother responded before I could barely get the words out.

"You want me to get up on that stand and tell everyone that I pimped my own goddamn daughter? No, I ain't doin' it. You got yourself into this mess, and it's up to you to fix it. You need to go on down there to that police station and ask for a deal while you still can."

Dana's father caught the tail-end of her mother's comment. He was shocked and dismayed by Diana's coldness.

"YOU did this to her, Diana. And now, you're refusing to help her? What kind of woman are you?"

"I'm a better woman than the one you got now. Believe that. She ain't nothing, but a junkie herself. Hell, she shot more dope back in the day than all of the junkie's combined. You, Cookie, and Dana can kiss my..."

"Momma, please. Forget I even mentioned it. Daddy, let's go."

"You go ahead. I need to have a word with Diana--in private."

"You sure?"

"Yeah, I'm sure. I'll be right out."

As Dana left the room, she could see the anger in her father's eyes and the pulsating veins in his neck. The last thing the family needed was another murder charge, Dana thought as she left the room. She posted up behind the closed hospital door, in case things got out of hand. She heard the entire conversation.

Chapter Twenty-Eight
Divine Intervention

"Diana, I think it's time for you to get some serious help. If you can't do it for yourself, then consider doing it for your daughter."

"How dare you come in here acting like you running things? If that's what you came in here to tell me, you can leave."

"No, that's not all I came in here to say. I came to remind you that you have three other children who need you. You haven't seen them in over six years, and you don't even call them. How do you think they feel? Or do you even care?"

For a moment, it seemed that he might have struck a nerve. Then, all of a sudden, Diana went into a violent rage.

"Get out! Now! And don't come back," she yelled and threw the bowl of fruit, just barely missing his face.

Alex

Within seconds, the nurses entered the room along with Dana and the rest of her family. Ken and I returned from the convenience store and were just in time to witness the commotion.

"Diana, calm down," Dana's grandmother pleaded.

"Then, tell him to stay the hell away from me!" she screamed.

One of the nurses injected her with a shot of an unknown medication through her IV. A few seconds later, she sat down in the recliner and focused her attention on the ceiling. Eventually, her eyes began to close and she appeared to be asleep.

Dana's Uncle Leonard shook his head.

"How long has she been like this? I had no idea it was this bad, but then again, it's been six years since I saw her. I should have followed my first mind and insisted on coming to check on her."

"At least you knew how to reach her, Leonard. Every number I had was disconnected and every letter I sent came back unopened."

Dana's grandmother replied in sadness.

"I didn't have a number. She just called periodically."

"Okay, so what are we going to do? She can't stay here in East Boogie."

Leonard appeared to be a take-action sort of guy, like his son.

"She'll go home with me. I'll take care of her."

Dana's grandmother seemed to have it all figured out. Somehow, I didn't think she was in any shape to deal with Diana.

"Granny, that's out of the question."

Dana must have read my mind.

"You haven't seen anything yet. It gets worse. Once the cravings kick in, a recovering junkie will do anything for a fix. I can't let you put yourself in that kind of danger."

"But she's my daughter..."

"Mother, I don't know who this person is, but it's not your daughter. I agree with Dana. She can't go home with you. She's coming with me."

"But Uncle Leonard..."

"No, I've got this. It's about time someone put an end to this nonsense. She'll come home with me and I'll get her into one of those treatment centers in Metairie."

The treating physician must have overheard a portion of the conversation as he walked through the door.

"I think now is a good time for us to discuss Mrs. Toussaint's condition moving forward. Please come with me."

Ken and turned to go to the waiting room, but Dana insisted that we come along as well. The doctor led us to a private conference room.

"I'm Dr. Raines. I'm the Chief of Critical Care and I'm also an addiction specialist. I've been taking care of Mrs. Toussaint since she was admitted. Who is the immediate next of kin?"

Everyone immediately turned to Dana and Dana looked at her father for help. He stepped forward with his arms crossed.

"It's a little complicated. I'm still married to Diana, but we've been separated for nearly twelve years."

Dana was under the impression that her parents were divorced, but she'd recently discovered that they were still married.

The doctor scribbled something on his pad and continued.

"What we have here is an extremely severe case of opioid addiction. It's not the worst I've seen, but it's pretty close. I went through her hospital record and this is her fourth admission for heroin overdose in the last six months with no documentation of prior admissions. This is a concern to me for a couple of reasons, but the immediate concern is related to the potency of the heroin currently on the street. It seems to have increased tremendously within the last year and this is consistent with the overall number of hospital admissions. With a long-standing addiction like Mrs. Toussaint's, it's just a matter of time before she encounters a lethal dose."

So Mr. James and Tyree were selling a "better" product. After years of getting high on the diluted stuff, junkies were overdosing like crazy.

"What are our options?"

My grandmother's voice sounded frail.

"Apparently, she's put forth some effort with the outpatient methadone treatment program without much success. The next logical step would be a long term in-patient treatment program, but in all honesty, I don't know if this option would be beneficial for her at this point."

"Why is that?"

Dana's uncle wanted to know.

"These particular programs tend to be less effective in individuals who are not completely sold on the idea of getting clean. After speaking with Mrs. Toussaint regarding her immediate plans, I didn't get the impression that she's there yet."

Complete silence. So far, there didn't appear to be any viable options. Dr. Raines cleared his throat.

"The last option is pretty extreme. Rapid detox is an experimental treatment for opioid addiction that requires admission to the intensive care unit and induction of general anesthesia. The patient undergoes a medication induced comatose state for a predetermined period of time and the most severe symptoms of withdrawal are completed while under general anesthesia. The treatment is still in the experimental phase, but so far the preliminary data is very promising."

"What about the anesthesia-related risks? Surely these patients aren't the best candidates for general anesthesia."

I handled a few anesthesia-related wrongful death cases, so I knew a little about the dangers of general anesthesia.

"You are correct. I have to be honest with you. The jury is still out concerning risks versus benefits, particularly from the anesthesia perspective. However, considering the alternatives, I'm still a proponent of this method."

"She'll never agree to it."

I could see that Dana had begun to re-think her plea. Her mother's testimony was her best chance to receive a not guilty verdict. Without it, I would definitely have my work cut out for her.

"Well, that brings me back to my initial question concerning the immediate next of kin. Due to Mrs. Toussaint's long-standing history of drug abuse and her recent admissions to the hospital, you may be able to obtain a medical power of attorney. This would give you the authority to make decisions on her behalf."

The doctor directed his comment to my father.

"But wouldn't she have to agree to it? There's no way in hell Diana would give me that kind of control."

Mr. Toussaint was absolutely correct in his assessment. Diana's pride would prevent her from agreeing to such a thing.

"Patient consent is the desired method of consent for medical power of attorney, but there are a couple of ways around it, Mr. Toussaint. If you can prove that she's a harm to herself or incapable of making appropriate health-related decisions, you may petition the court for an involuntary commission for inpatient care."

"Is that something like a coroner's commission?"

Dana's Uncle Leonard frowned at the doctor. Apparently, the "coroner's commission" was pretty common in Louisiana.

"Yes, sir it is."

"A coroner's commission is usually good for up to seventy-two hours. What is the required treatment time for rapid detox?"

I asked the doctor the question as a spark of hope lit within my mind. This could actually work, I thought. If we could get Diana clean and keep her clean for at least a hundred and sixty-one days, she might agree to testify.

"Good question, Ms..."

"Phillips."

"Ms. Phillips. The high-risk portion of the procedure, which is general anesthesia, may be completed within four to twelve hours. The treating physician would determine the patient-specific length of time upon admission."

The seventy-two hour commission would be more than enough time.

"I've given you an enormous amount of information in a really short time. I have to be honest with you, time is of the essence. Mrs. Toussaint won't survive another overdose of this magnitude. Those are your options from a treatment standpoint. Please take some time to think about it and don't hesitate to contact me if you have additional questions. Here's my card and a list of the treatment facilities that I would personally recommend, as well as some additional information regarding rapid detox."

"Thanks, Dr. Raines," Mrs. Ledoux whispered.

"Not a problem, ma'am."

Dana was the first to speak after the doctor left the room.

"You have the legal right to make decisions," Dana said to her father, "but I think Granny should have the final say."

"I totally agree, Dana," her father replied grimly.

Leonard nodded his agreement as well.

"Granny, what do you want to do?"

"I don't think we have much of a choice," Mrs. Ledoux stated matter-of-factly.

"You want the rapid detox?"

"From the looks of it, that's our only option. It's only by the grace of the good Lord that she survived this time..."

"CODE BLUE, CODE BLUE."

The intercom system interrupted Mrs. Ledoux. A few seconds later, one of the nurses entered the conference room.

"Mrs. Toussaint was just found unresponsive in her room. The code team is working to resuscitate her..."

"What happened? She was fine when we left," Leonard was upset with the news like everyone else.

"Sir, we don't have any answers yet. Right now, the priority is getting her stabilized and then we'll figure out what happened."

"I need to see her."

Dana's grandmother handled the news well, but it was just a matter of time before her emotional strength finally depleted.

"Ma'am, we can't let you in the room at this time. Please bear with us."

Within a matter of minutes, the family was presented with another ordeal. This one more serious than any of the previous concerns. Dana's grandmother began to pray as we all stood in a circle and held hands. It was the "Our Father's Prayer." Each word was spoken with such passion that it seemed like it was written specifically for this occasion.

"...lead us not into temptation, but deliver us from evil. For thine is the kingdom, the power and the glory, Amen."

Dr. Raines was present when we opened our eyes. No one said a word for fear of hearing the worst.

"She's stable, but we had to place her back on the breathing machine."

"So, this couldn't have been a drug overdose. What happened?" Dana's father asked.

"We are pretty certain she's suffered some damage to the right side of her heart as a result of the intravenous drug use. The condition is called endocarditis, which is basically an infection along the lining of the heart. If left untreated, the condition can lead to the formation of blood clots in the lungs. The blood clot in the lungs is what caused the respiratory arrest and subsequent placement on the breathing machine."

"What's the prognosis?"

I knew it was serious, but I wanted to know if there was any hope for survival.

"The immediate danger is the blood clot to the lung, but it can be managed with medication. Our biggest concern is the infection and the overall damage to her heart."

"What's the worst case scenario?" Dana asked.

"Worst case scenario is possible replacement of one the valves in her heart with open heart surgery. We won't know the extent of the damage until all of the tests are complete."

"How long will that take?"

Mrs. Ledoux asked the question as she sat heavily into a chair.

"Three to five days."

"The Lord works in mysterious ways. If she's on that machine for that amount of time, there's no need for the rapid detox."

"Well, that's certainly a perspective I hadn't considered. You're right, Mrs. Ledoux. If and when she's taken off the breathing machine, the acute phase of withdrawal will be over."

The frown lines suddenly left Mrs. Ledoux's forehead.

"You know, I've been taking care of addicts for over fifteen years. I can honestly say that nearly all of the ones who actually make it are the ones who hit rock bottom. If this isn't rock bottom, I don't know what is," the physician said before he left the room.

Chapter Twenty-Nine
When People Show You Who They Are, Believe Them

Alex

The damage to Diana's heart was extensive enough to warrant surgery and surprisingly, she came through with flying colors. The way things were going, Mrs. Ledoux was correct in her analysis of the situation. The setback was a blessing in disguise. Diana remained in a medically induced coma for close to ten days, which was needed to optimize her health in preparation for open-heart surgery. It was more than enough time for her body to go through the detoxification phase and in the process, Diana would be spared the horrible effects of withdrawal. Her prognosis after the surgery wasn't the greatest, but the mere fact that she survived was additional proof that miracles do happen. When she was strong enough to travel, they transferred her to a physical rehabilitation facility in Metarie, Louisiana, which was close to her family. The facility also offered addiction management services.

Dana's family was convinced that Diana would willingly testify on Dana's behalf once she completed the drug rehabilitation program. However, this was yet to be confirmed. As a result, I decided to proceed with caution and prepare the main element of the case with the assumption that Diana would not be the key witness. This approach would require an extensive amount of digging which was already underway. I looked for the type of jaw dropping evidence that Latrice managed to bring forth in Yasmin's case. I knew the chances of getting a tape recorded confession from the deceased was slim to none, but I was determined to find something.

Since Dana insisted that my wedding had to take place prior to the trial, I was in the process of planning my wedding as well. On top of that, I still had to figure out how to tell Lawrence that I was engaged. Ken suggested we tell him together, however, I didn't think that was such a good idea. Somehow, complex situations always seem to work themselves out. It was time for Jordan's two-week visit to Florida with his dad. Ken was at my house when Lawrence arrived, which was a first. Strategic planning on my part prevented any encounters between the two of them until that day.

Ken gave me a look and I knew exactly what he thought. I took a deep breath and decided to let him handle it. I excused myself to gather Jordan's things for the trip. I figured it was best if Jordan didn't hear the conversation and to be honest, I didn't want to hear it either.

I took more time than I really needed, for obvious reasons, and I could tell Jordan was a little anxious.

"Mommy, let's go. I'm ready to go with Daddy."

"Okay, Sweetie, I think I have everything."

At three and a half, Jordan had begun to cling to his dad more and more. Lawrence and I were both a couple of losers for not making things work, but at this point, it was water under the bridge. I moved on and I suspected he would do the same.

"Let's go."

We walked back into the living room and Jordan immediately grabbed his dad's hand.

"Bye-bye, Mommy."

"See you later, sweetie. Be good."

"I will Mommy, I'm a big boy."

I sat the suitcase and duffle bag down by the door and waited for him to say something but he didn't. Lawrence slowly picked up the bags and grabbed Jordan's hand. He left without saying a word.

"So, how did it go?"

"Not well, but under the circumstances, I'm not surprised. Alex, he says you never told him you were seeing someone. He was under the impression that things were "good" between the two of you. So now, I'm confused. Why didn't you tell him about us, Alex?"

"It's not what you think Ken. It just never seemed like the right time. I know it doesn't make a whole lot of sense, but it's the truth."

"I'm getting a bad vibe about this. The guy is crushed. He says you haven't been honest with him and that he thought things were okay. He mentioned some guy named Demetrius..."

"Demetrius?"

I repeated the name in confusion. What in the world did Demetrius have to do with any of this? He thought things were okay? Really? That statement alone convinced me that something was seriously wrong with Lawrence. How could things be okay when we rarely even communicated about anything other than travel arrangements for Jordan?

"He said you 'pulled a stunt' like this before and that you didn't go through with it because you were still in love with him."

"Wow, what an egotistical bastard. My decision not to marry Demetrius was more about me and where I was emotionally. I walked away from that relationship because I was confused and afraid."

"Afraid of what?"

"Making a mistake..."

"Did you love him?"

"Yes."

I was glad he didn't ask me to specify because I didn't think I could adequately explain how I managed to be in love with two people at the same time.

"So, what happened?'

"I was in a long distance relationship with Lawrence when I met Demetrius. I made it perfectly clear that I was not interested in anything other than friendship. However, I was extremely vulnerable and frustrated when I met him and I think he recognized it. I spent the first few months trying to convince Demetrius that things were okay between Lawrence and I, but I wasn't really sure myself. Demetrius did all of the right things and eventually, I ended my relationship with Lawrence. Shortly after that, I realized I wasn't at peace with my decision and I ended my relationship with Demetrius as well."

"I'm confused."

"I know it doesn't make sense, but I just couldn't get past the fact that I betrayed Lawrence and that my relationship with Demetrius was built on lies."

"Where is this guy now?"

"Happily married."

"I hate to tell you this, Alex, but there's not much difference in the way you handled that situation and the way you handled this one."

"I love you, Ken, and for once in my life, I'm at peace--no reservations."

"Are you sure?"

"Absolutely."

Dana

I had less than four months of freedom before the trial and I was more depressed than I'd ever been in my life. However, my husband wasn't having it. He insisted that we proceed with everything, excluding the honeymoon, as planned. We moved into our new house with the boys and tried to live a normal life for as long as we could.

Mack settled into his new role as Amina's manager and made some major moves. Amina had already met with one of the record labels that J-Street mentioned. To my surprise, she turned down a lucrative deal with the company because it excluded her "management team."

"Amina, that was the deal you've been waiting for. You would have had my blessings if you had taken it."

"Too late. I already said no. We started this thing together and that's how I plan to roll. If you hadn't pushed me, I would have given up and all of my dreams would have died behind those prison walls. Take a look at this."

She handed me a contract from the other record label. This one was based in Houston.

"It's legit, and almost as good as the first one."

While Amina wrote her lyrics in the prison library, I read everything I could get my hands on that pertained to the business side of the music industry. The contract contained the type of language we wanted and much more. The contract was worth millions.

"I know. I just need my manager to sign it."

I could count the number of friends I had throughout my entire life on one hand and each of them shared the same trait-- loyalty. I was absolutely convinced that it's better to have four quarters than a hundred pennies. The contract was signed and Amina was on her way.

Alex's wedding was beautiful. Unlike me, she had tons of friends and her sorority sisters represented well for the occasion. Alex chose me to be her matron of honor and her friend Camilla served as the maid of honor. We were both honored to stand for a friend like Alex.

The color scheme for her wedding was a no-brainer. There were splashes of salmon pink and apple green all over the church and the bride's maid dresses were a beautiful floral combination of the two colors. The bride and groom prepared their own wedding vows and their words were simple, but the meaning was undeniable. Fate and destiny brought them back together again after so many years and they planned to spend the rest of their lives making up for lost time.

According to Alex, Lawrence was in denial until the very end and devastated when he realized she was determined to move on with Ken.

"I loved him, Dana, but I felt like I was doing it from a distance. There was always some type of obstacle between us. By the time Ken came along again, I was content with being alone for the rest of my life and I kept telling myself I was okay with that. Apparently, I was wrong. I'm happier than I've ever been in my life and I'm at peace."

After the wedding, they were off to the Caribbean for a quick honeymoon, and from there, she and Ken would meet us in East St Louis. It was time to decide my fate.

Chapter Thirty
A Mother's Love

Alex

Diana completed the physical rehabilitation and was focused on the addiction rehabilitation portion of the program. From everything I'd ever heard about heroin addiction, I was pretty sure the physical rehab was a cakewalk compared to kicking a heroin habit. I was relieved when I learned that the family would receive counseling to help them understand the complexity of Diana's journey. Addiction is a symptom of an underlying issue. In order for Diana to completely overcome her demons, she would have to acknowledge those issues and share them with her family. Within the first six steps of the twelve-step program, Diana would have an opportunity to do just that. While those steps were important, I was a little skeptical about the way Diana would handle steps eight and nine:

8. Make a list of all persons we harmed and make amends to them all.

9. Make direct amends to such people wherever possible, except when to do so would injure them or others.

As it turns out, my concerns were valid. Diana's "list" was terribly incomplete because she failed to include the one person that should have been included above all others--Dana. Not only did she exclude her from the list, she refused to talk about her dealings with Mr. James at all. I was glad that I followed my instincts and began my search for an alternate "star witness" early on. At this point, I was sure that Diana would not take the stand in her daughter's defense.

The trial began on May 29, which was a dreary Monday. It also marked Dana's four-month wedding anniversary. I felt sad for her that she would spend it in a courtroom.

In his opening statement, the prosecutor had the audacity to suggest that in spite of his criminal occupation, "Mr. James was still a compassionate human being who didn't deserve to have his life taken in such a cruel manner." He went on to cite a number of monetary contributions to various community charities over the years and vowed to further prove this claim through witness testimony. Other than Mr. James' mother, I couldn't think of anyone in the city who would be willing to offer such testimony under oath. The prosecution's first witness would solve the mystery. Bishop Richard Blake was the pastor and founder of New Eastside Living Ministries, which was one of the largest and most affluent churches in East Boogie. Apparently, his organization was a huge recipient of Mr. James' benevolence and the pastor provided a detailed list of monetary contributions. When he took the stand, Dana lost it. She screamed obscenities at the pastor, and I was barely able to keep her in her seat. At the end of the testimony, Dana stood up when he walked by the defense table.

"How dare you come in here and lie in front of all of these people. Why didn't you tell the whole story?"

The judge slammed his gavel to stop Dana's outburst.

"Order in the court! This court is in recess! Attorney Phillips, you have fifteen minutes to get your client under control. If you can't, she will be held in contempt and banned from the remainder of these proceedings."

"Yes, your honor."

I grabbed Dana's arm and pulled her into her chair.

"Dana, can you tell me what just happened?"

"That bastard could be Isaiah's father, Alex. And he had the nerve to get on that witness stand and pretend that James was a saint..."

"Whoa, slow down, Dana. Are you telling me that you slept with him?"

"Yes! He was one of the men that James brought to the house. He wasn't the only one. I should have put a bullet in his head when he showed up at Ja'El's funeral."

Dana went on to fill me in some of the missing pieces from her past concerning Mr. James. Not only did he traffic drugs, but he was also trafficked girls.

"Dana, if there were more men involved, what makes you think this man is Isaiah's father?"

"He and James were the only two that didn't use condoms. If James could produce children, I would have been pregnant long before Isaiah came along. He was sterile."

"We need a DNA sample."

"I doubt if he'll..."

"He doesn't have to. I need you to stay calm, Dana. Please. We're doing extremely well so far, but you have to hold it together."

"I know. I'm okay. Seeing him just took me by surprise. It won't happen again."

The new information gave me an idea. If it worked, Dana would be able to put this behind her and move on once and for all.

The prosecutor had a couple of other surprises that I didn't expect. The next two witnesses were ladies who claimed to be Dana's co-workers at the strip club. Their testimonies were obviously designed to mar Dana's character even further. It was an excellent move, but the prosecutor didn't cover all of the bases on this particular topic. Little did he know, the move would actually work in the favor of the defense.

The prosecution rested their case on the first day, which was earlier than I anticipated. I was ready for cross-examination the next morning, but I had some issues to address before I called the defense's first witness. My private investigator managed to locate a young lady that had the misfortune of meeting Mr. James when she was in junior high school. Like Dana, she had a child at an early age as well. I had already submitted DNA samples for her child, along with Dana's son in hopes that both samples would be matched to Mr. James. This was supposed to be the jaw dropping evidence that would set Dana free, but after my conversation with Dana, those chances were slim to none. I needed to speak with the young lady to see if her story was consistent with Dana's story regarding the use of condoms. If the preacher and Mr. James were the only two men that didn't use condoms, there was a remote possibility that the preacher was the father of both children. If this was the case, my plan was to include him as a hostile witness and expose the entire human trafficking operation. This testimony alone would be enough to plant a seed of doubt for the jurors. The only foreseeable obstacle was getting a sample of the preacher's DNA. I would cross that bridge when we got there. At that point, I had to focus on my meeting with our star witness.

"Erica, thanks for all of your help. I appreciate your willingness to serve as a witness on behalf of my client."

"No problem. Dana and I went to the same school. She was a couple of years ahead of me, but I remember her."

"Were you aware of her relationship with Mr. James at the time?"

"Not at first, but I figured it out. No one in East Boogie could afford to wear nice clothes and shoes to school every day. After I hooked up with Mr. James, he started buying me all of these nice things. That's when I realized Dana and all of the other girls with named brand stuff were involved with him as well. No one told me and I never saw it, I just knew."

"How did you meet Mr. James?"

"He just showed up at our house one day and my mother told me he was there to pick me up."

It was identical to Dana's story.

"Erica, I need to ask you something. Was your mother using drugs at the time?"

"My mother was a crackhead."

Her voice broke, but she took a deep breath and continued.

Erica had two sisters and two brothers. She was the oldest. What she described was something I simply couldn't imagine. She said her mother was once the secretary at the elementary school and that one day, she just didn't come home from work. She spent three days in a crack house and left her five kids alone to fend for themselves. When her mother came home she was never the same. The four younger kids eventually went to live with her grandmother. She said there were times when her mother didn't come home for weeks, but she went to school every day because it was the only way she'd have anything to eat. By the time Mr. James came along, she had given up on things getting better and her only desire in life was to have a decent meal and a coat for winter. At first, she saw her relationship with him as the answer to her prayers. She viewed the sexual part of the relationship as a well-deserved means to an end. Her views changed when Mr. James began to pass her around to his friends. When she protested, he used verbal restraint. Over time, her self-worth and optimism for a better life were replaced by dependence and submission. When she got pregnant, he dropped her like a hot potato because he said that she was useless.

Behind Closed Doors: *Dana's Story*

"So, what did you do?"

"I turned myself in to child protective services because I had nowhere else to go and I couldn't take care of my child."

"What about your grandmother?"

"She said it was too late for me. I was already destined to be just like my mother."

"So, how did you manage to survive? What about the baby?"

"I was placed in a good foster home with a family that did right by me. I finished high school and took the eighteen-month course to become a vocational nurse. I left East Boogie before the ink dried on the diploma."

"We're lucky to even find you."

"You have my foster parents to thank for that."

"Erica, who is your baby's father?"

"If I had to guess, I'd say the jack-legged preacher is Darby's father."

"Are you sure?"

"Yes, I'm sure."

"How do you know?"

"My child is the splitting image of that man."

"One more question, Erica, where's your mother?"

"Dead...massive heart attack at the age of thirty-six."

Cross-examination began the next morning. I called the two ex-strippers first. My goal was to buy myself enough time to get the DNA results back from a lab in Chicago. My detective hand delivered the samples and was instructed to wait for the results. For a hefty fee, the lab was able to guarantee the results within twenty-four hours.

My detective entered the courtroom at exactly five p.m. I quickly requested a fifteen-minute recess and hurried to his side.

"Please, tell me you have good news."

"I have good news. It's a match."

I had to sit down for fear of fainting. Without a match, the whole case was dead in the water.

Before re-entering the courtroom, I took a moment to prepare Dana for what was about to happen.

"Dana, we've located a witness that is prepared to testify on your behalf. She's one of Mr. James' victims, but that's not all. She has a daughter. Dana, her daughter and your son have the same father."

"Who is it?"

"She thinks it's Richard Blake."

"Is she sure?"

"Yes, she's pretty sure. If we can get the judge to order a DNA test for the preacher, he'll be forced to come clean about Mr. James and his role in brokering your services for his friends."

"I don't know what to say. This is too much."

"Listen, Dana, if we can make this happen, you'll walk out of here a free woman. If the judge refuses to order the DNA test or if the test is negative, we're in trouble."

"Do you have a plan B if either of those things happened?"

"Yes, your mother's testimony is the backup plan. If we can't get her to testify, I'll have to put you on the witness stand."

"She'll never do it. I'm prepared to testify."

The court session was scheduled to end at six p.m., but I was sure the session would be adjourned a little early once I got the preacher on the stand. After the judge reminded him that he was still under oath, I didn't waste any time with my attack.

"Reverend Blake, would you consider providing the court with a sample of your DNA?"

"Objection!"

The prosecutor screamed his outrage, and the courtroom erupted in dismay.

"Attorney Phillips, approach the bench."

The red-faced prosecutor quickly followed suit.

I was going for the shock effect. It worked.

"Your honor, please let me explain. I'm holding DNA test results from my client's son along with the results of another child. The children share the same biological father. My client and the other child's mother both claim that Reverend Blake fathered their children."

"This is not a paternity test hearing, Attorney Phillips, this is a murder case," the prosecutor stated sarcastically.

"Thanks for the reminder, sir, but I'm very much aware of that. Your honor, establishing the paternity of these children is vital to my client's case. Reverend Blake has first-hand knowledge of the decedent's involvement in the trafficking of under-aged girls which was the driving force behind my client's actions."

"Attorney Phillips, if you're interested in bringing charges against the reverend, you should consider filing a formal complaint."

I stopped myself from an eye roll at the prosecutor's asinine statement.

"That's for me to decide," the judge stated firmly.

"Attorney Phillips, if I were to order the DNA testing and your client and the witness are wrong, are you prepared to handle the consequences?"

The judge's implication was clear. If the DNA results were negative, the entire case could be compromised in the eyes of the jury. I had already discussed this with Dana, and we had an alternate plan.

"We are, your honor."

"Very well. I will order the test and expedite the results."

The prosecutor and I returned to our respective positions.

"Court is adjourned until 3 p.m. tomorrow afternoon."

I decided it was time for a family meeting. Dana was up to speed with the defense strategy, but in light of the impending bombshell, I figured the family should be prepared as well. After dinner, we met in the conference room of the hotel where everyone lodged during the trial.

After I brought them up to speed on the recent developments in the case, there was complete silence. Miss Cookie shook her head in disbelief and Dana's grandmother was visibly shaken.

"What kind of a place is this? The preacher running around making babies with underage girls, mothers on drugs, and the drug dealer pimping their children. This is no place to raise a child."

Mrs. Ledoux was the first to speak.

"No, it's not," Dana softly agreed.

"This is my fault. I never should have brought my family to this hell hole."

Mr. Toussaint did not handle the information well at all. If Dana was convicted, it would destroy him for sure.

"Listen, we can't change the past. We have to move forward. If things go as planned and the DNA is a match, the case is pretty much closed. Without a match, things could go the opposite direction. Up until now, I've tried to build Dana's case without her mother's testimony. If by chance the DNA is not a match, we may need it."

"She's still refusing, but I think if it came down to it, I can get her to testify."

I was relieved by Leonard's confident response.

"Well, that's all I have for now. Court is at three, so get some rest. We still have a full day of testimony in spite of the late start. I'll see you guys tomorrow."

Ken and I headed for the door. Dana's Uncle J.P. stopped us in our tracks.

"Thanks, Alex, for taking this case. Your passion is very obvious and I know that Dana wouldn't have gotten that with anyone else."

His words made me smile.

"You're welcome, Mr. Toussaint. I'm determined to get her back home to her boys."

Ken and I made it back to the room and out of nowhere, I found myself locked in an extremely passionate kiss.

"What was that for," I asked breathlessly.

"Because I love you and because you are an incredible woman. I knew it the first time I laid eyes on you."

"I love you too, Ken. I thought I was strong, but you give me strength that I never knew I had."

"How so?"

"Just being here, and just knowing that you support me. It's something that I've never experienced."

"Well, in that case, get ready to conquer the world because I'm not going anywhere."

The DNA test confirmed Dana and Erica's suspicions. The good reverend was the father of both children.

Chapter Thirty-One
Moral Justice

The DNA results were read to the jury.

"Reverend Blake, can you provide an explanation for the DNA results? And remember you are under oath?"

As if on cue, he broke down and cried like a baby.

"It was the devil...the devil made me do it! This is my "thorn in the side.""

He wailed dramatically.

"Thorn in the side? Your attraction for underage girls is your thorn in the side? That's your excuse?"

Unbelievable. He used the Bible to explain his depravity.

After the dramatic outburst, I asked him to recount his relationship with Mr. James concerning the underage girls.

"I never asked where the girls came from. We just had an understanding. On certain days of the week, I would arrive at his house at an appointed time and he would have a girl there waiting for me."

"How much did you pay for each encounter?"

"Eight hundred dollars."

"How many times per week?"

"Once, maybe twice a week."

"So, you paid the decedent $800-$1,600 dollars per week for underage girls."

"Yes."

More tears and sobs.

"So, you were having sex with minors on a regular basis? Was your wife aware of this?"

"No, she was not."

"Did you use condoms, Reverend Blake?"

"No, I did not."

"Did you ever consider the possibility of contracting a sexually transmitted disease or the possibility of producing children with young ladies who were just children themselves?"

"They were young. James told me they couldn't get pregnant. He also said his other clients were required to use condoms. He said I didn't have to."

So the Reverend got a pass on the condoms because he was a "man of the cloth." The more questions I asked, the more disgusted I became with the situation.

I'd heard enough and I was sure the jurors heard enough as well. I could see the disgust on each of their faces. Miss Cookie was the next witness. Dana was fourteen when she moved in with Miss Cookie. Her testimony was used to further establish a timeline and to emphasize Dana's unstable and traumatic home life. Her testimony was followed by the former owner of the strip club. The prosecutor's decision to rely on a couple of strippers for compelling evidence was a dangerous move. According to Dana, Mr. James was responsible for her employment at the strip club and was compensated for his efforts. I had my private investigator to track down the owner of the club to get his side of the story. His testimony would negate anything the two women had to say.

"Sir, can you summarize your business relationship with Mr. Harris?"

The former club owner was not in the best health and looked much older than his actual age. His olive skin had just a hint of a yellow hue to it and his eyes had a yellow tinge as well.

"Mr. Harris was a regular at my club. One night, he approached me with a photo of a young lady and asked if I would be interested in her services at my club."

"Is the young lady present in the courtroom?"

"She's sitting right there," he said and pointed to Dana.

"Did you give her a job?"

"Yes, I did. I thought she was the prettiest girl I'd ever seen."

"Did he tell you that she was underage?"

"No, he did not. And to be honest, I didn't ask. I assumed she was of age. I was just eager to get her in my club because I knew she would bring in tons of business."

"Did you compensate Mr. Harris for his efforts?"

"Yes, I did. He got a thousand dollars each time she entered the building."

"No further questions."

As it turns out, the club owner suffered from Hepatitis induced cirrhosis of the liver. After years of shooting heroin, he finally got clean, but the damage was already done. His slow and painful death was also compliments of Mr. James. Undoubtedly, this was his motivation for testifying on Dana's behalf.

Erica was my final witness. Hers would consume the most time because my goal was to allow her to recount all of the information she'd given me that concerned her mother's addiction and the subsequent impact on her family. Her testimony clearly painted the picture of a man who preyed on poor, struggling women who used drugs to escape the harsh realities of life in a dead end city. Their dependence on drugs ultimately led to their dependence on Mr. James. Erica's testimony established a consistent pattern of behavior for Mr. James. The women were strategically selected and targeted for one purpose--their daughters. After Erica's testimony, I was convinced more than ever that the love of money was the root of all evil, however, poverty and lack were its greatest companions. The women and children of East St Louis were doomed from the very beginning and the circle was far from being broken. Somehow, Erica managed to beat the odds.

I rested my case with confidence and patiently sat through the cross-examination, which was short and sweet. The brevity of a cross-examination was always a positive indicator for the defense attorney. It was the first sign of surrender for the prosecution. Closing arguments began the next morning. Like the cross-examination, the prosecution's closing arguments were brief as well. In all honesty, his words seemed forced and it was apparent to me that if given the task, he probably would have voted not guilty right along with the jury.

The jury returned with a verdict in record time. Dana was found not guilty. Her nightmare was finally over.

Epilogue

When all was said and done, there were a number of reasons to be thankful. For starters, a pedophiliac pimp/drug dealer was off the street and a tainted minister was exposed. The human trafficking ring that managed to operate in visible obscurity for so many years was finally a thing of the past. In all, thirty men were arrested. During the investigation, detectives discovered evidence to prove that some of the girls were taken across the bridge to St. Louis, which made the crime a federal offense. The Mann Act of 1912 was designed to impose a felony for the interstate trafficking and prostitution of women or girls under the age of eighteen. For victims under the age of fourteen, the penalty is fifteen years to life. Dana and Erica were both under the age of fourteen when their abuse began. As a result, Reverend Blake would serve a minimum of fifteen years in prison.

Everyone was overjoyed with the outcome of the trial, but unfortunately, this would not be the end of the suffering for Dana's family. Diana was found dead from a heroin overdose a few weeks after the trial. A photo of Dana as an infant, was found beside her body along with a note that contained the words that Dana had never heard from her mother, "I love you, Dana."

Diana was diagnosed with a mental condition called borderline personality disorder during her stay at the drug rehab facility. The symptoms of borderline personality disorder usually appear during the teenage years and early twenties. In hindsight, Dana's grandmother said she noticed a distinct change in her daughter's behavior a couple of years after she graduated from high school. The angry outbursts and extreme rebellion seemed to escalate on a daily basis, and Mrs. Ledoux was convinced that her daughter was using drugs. That was partially true, however, Diana began to use drugs in order to mask the symptoms of her disease. Individuals with borderline personality disorder are prone to unstable interpersonal relationships and have difficulty focusing on the feelings of others because their own emotional pain is too great.

Mourning the loss of a mother who had been the source of so much pain in her life was an extremely difficult task. However, Dana finally had an explanation for her mother's behavior and it wasn't voodoo as Miss Angélique suggested so many years ago. It was mental illness.

About The Author

Dr. A.L. Smith read her first full-length novel (The Boxcar Children, by Gertrude Chandler Warner) in the third grade and it spawned her passion for reading. Authors who have influenced her the most include Sister Souljah, Iceberg Slim (Robert Beck), Donald Goines, Nathan McCall, Zora Neal Hurston, Dr. Frances Cress Welsing, Claud Brown, Cynthia Middlebrooks Harris, E. Lynn Harris and Treasure Blue to name a few. According to Dr. Smith, the hallmark of a great story is the resounding presence of a character that transcends the final pages of the book.

Dr. Smith is a native of Frierson, Louisiana, a small town in northeast Louisiana with a population of 148 residents. She attended Grambling State University on a basketball scholarship and later joined the school's Army ROTC program. Upon graduation in 1996, she became the university's first Army ROTC cadet to receive a commission in the Army Nurse Corps. She received a Masters Degree in Nurse Anesthesia in 2001 and a Doctorate of Nurse Anesthesia Practice in 2012 from Texas Wesleyan University. Her doctoral research project was selected for inclusion in the 2016 edition of the Journal of Gastroenterology Nursing.

In 2010, she participated in humanitarian relief efforts during the devastating earthquake in Haiti and provided anesthesia services to a countless number of victims, many of whom were children. This experience would have a profound impact on her views concerning socioeconomic disparities here in the U.S. and countries abroad. She's a member of Alpha Kappa Alpha Sorority, Inc. and takes seriously the organization's motto "Service to all Mankind". Her personal motto is "In as much as you've done to the least of the..."

www.ingramcontent.com/pod-product-compliance
Lightning Source LLC
LaVergne TN
LVHW021704060526
838200LV00050B/2492